# CORPORATE MAGICK

# CORPORATE MAGICK

## Mystical Tools for Business Success

# BOB JOHNSON

CITADEL PRESS
Kensington Publishing Corp.
www.kensingtonbooks.com

CITADEL PRESS BOOKS are published by

Kensington Publishing Corp.
850 Third Avenue
New York, NY 10022

All Kensington titles, imprints, and distributed lines are available at special quantity discounts for bulk purchases for sales promotions, premiums, fund-raising, and educational, or institutional use. Special book excerpts or customized printings can also be created to fit specific needs. For details, write or phone the office of the Kensington special sales manager: Kensington Publishing Corp., 850 Third Avenue, New York, NY 10022, attn: Special Sales Department, phone 1-800-221-2647.

CITADEL PRESS is Reg. U.S. Pat. & TM Off.
The Citadel Logo is a trademark of Kensington Publishing Corp.

Designed by Leonard Telesca

First Printing: November 2002

10 9 8 7 6 5 4 3 2 1

Printed in the United States of America

Library of Congress Control Number 2002110565

ISBN 0-8065-2393-X

*For TinaMarie,*
*who brings me magick every day.*

# Contents

**Preface**                   xi

**INTRODUCTION**
**Mystical Tools for Business Success**     xv
     A magickal primer on *how* and *why* magick works in
     business, and a brief look at how the different occult
     disciplines can make you a success by using affirmations,
     meditation, and other magickal and mental exercises.

**CHAPTER 1**
**The Ivy League of Magick**             3
     A look at the different magickal disciplines that make up
     the basis of *Corporate Magick,* including witchcraft,
     Santeria, voodoo, astrology, Kabbalah, and others, and
     why elements of each have specific business applications.

**CHAPTER 2**
**Preparing the Magician**            23
     A how-to on preparing physically and mentally for
     casting spells and using awesome *Corporate Magick*
     tools. Exercises from different disciplines are included.

## CHAPTER 3
**The Corporate Hex-executive—Casting Spells
the Wiccan Way**                                      **40**

Actual witchcraft spells and their ingredients modified
for business use. What each spell can do for you, and
how and when to cast them.

## CHAPTER 4
**Talismans, Charms, and Amulets**                    **61**

Your favorite pen can be a magickal instrument, and
you'll be surprised at what else can work business
magick. Find out the secrets of talismans—what they
do, and how to make them.

## CHAPTER 5
**Astrology—Success by the Stars**                    **75**

How to pick stocks, companies, and people to further
your bank account and your career, all by charting the
stars.

## CHAPTER 6
**Voodoo—Get Your *Mojo* Working**                    **90**

Voodoo ceremonies, spells, and spirits to help you get
ahead. Dances, charms, and even the sun can help you
get that promotion or raise.

## CHAPTER 7
**Santeria for Success**                              **105**

Food, candles, and even some saints combine in this
Afro-Caribbean magickal system for material gain and,
when necessary, revenge.

## CHAPTER 8
**The Kabbalah—Become a Master of the Universe**      **126**

The ancient Hebrew magickal system is easier to use
than you think. How the Tree of Life works to help
your bottom line.

## CHAPTER 9
## Tools of Your Trade—Candles, Herbs, and
## Incense Magick

147

Three basic, but essential magickal tools—available
everywhere—can become your most powerful assistants.

## CHAPTER 10
## How to Be a God at Your Company

161

Using the power of suggestion and appearance to
create your magickal persona. How to be recognized
as someone with "powers" far beyond good business
sense.

## CHAPTER 11
## What They'd *Never* Teach at Harvard Business School:
## The Author's Personal Story

180

The real-life testimony from the author himself explaining how he used magick to secure a major position with
a New York publishing firm and many other business
triumphs.

## Appendix: Resources

191

Resources for recipes and how to create ingredients for
items used in spells, candles, talismans, charms, and oils.

## Bibliography

197

## Index

203

# Preface

You hold a powerful business tool in your hands. In fact, it's more than powerful, it's magickal! It may not look like any magickal instrument you've ever seen before, but it contains the wisdom and occult knowledge of some of the most incredible esoteric disciplines and mystery schools ever discovered. And now the secrets of this magick have been gathered, massaged, and customized to work specifically in all areas of the business world—*your* business world. Whether you're a corporate executive, manager, supervisor, rising star, or owner of your own business, *Corporate Magick: Mystical Tools for Business Success* will help you reach your goals by using spells, talismans, amulets, candles, powders, and the most awesome magickal weapon in your entire arsenal—*your mind.*

The beauty of *Corporate Magick* is that it works! I have documented many actual case studies of corporate magicians—people just like you and me who have tapped the power of magick and made it work for their careers and businesses. In fact, I tell my own story of success and how using magick allows me to live on two coasts and drive a Mercedes sports car.

What you'll find on these pages are practical, pragmatic instructions on using magick for ultimate success. Just for starters, you'll learn how to increase your worth in your company by using simple candle magick. You'll discover how to increase sales by using the ancient methods of the Kabbalah, *and* you can get that raise, promotion, or raise capital for your start-up business with the help of witchcraft and voodoo magick. Never before has magick been boiled down into such a simple-to-use manual strictly for the world of commerce. You won't be bogged down by the complicated rituals and ceremonies you'll find in almost every other book on magick, but you will get the benefit of the wisdom of master sorcerers and mages. The *Corporate Magick* system of magick has been developed for one reason, and one reason only—to help you succeed in your career and to improve your livelihood.

A radical departure from the regular occult world? Yes. But a departure whose time has come. And with all due respect to the many masters of the occult who've penned wonderful books on every subject, I feel we haven't diligently concentrated on making money. Magick's been used for thousands of years for gain and protection, so why not really focus on what's most important to almost everyone, every day of our lives? Well, that's what I've done.

*Corporate Magick* contains Instant Magickal Index Cards in every chapter that you can use immediately, even if you don't want to read the entire chapter. What's more, myself and a number of my colleagues have joined together to form the *Corporate Magick* Cabal—a group of magicians, psychics, and experts who will be telepathically connected to the readers of this book twenty-four hours a day, seven days a week, to bolster spells and help with all types of magick. You cast your spell and the Cabal assists you!

You'll also be able to get the latest information on spells, psychic stock predictions, and all manner of using magick in business from the *Corporate Magick* Web site at www.corporate magick.com.

You may ask why I use the term "corporate" in the title of this book when there is a whole world of business that functions outside of the corporate world. Well, the answer is simple. I feel that regardless of what area of commerce we talk about in the United States (and the U.S. does influence the world), corporations either control a good deal of the economic structure or play a major part in it somewhere down the line, from car manufacturers right down to the mom-and-pop clothing shop. Corporations somehow affect *everyone* who earns a living in America. And that's the kind of magick we need to tap.

Just a word about the use of gender in the book. I chose to use the masculine case simply for a smoother read and nothing else. As you'll see from the case studies, there are many, many women who are key people in the business world today, and by no means do I consider them any less important. There's no gender preference on the astral plane.

So, start making magick and becoming the tycoon you always knew you could be. You still need to work hard, but now you'll have an edge, an assistant, a force that's real but unseen. And you know as well as I do that in business today you need every advantage you can get.

# INTRODUCTION

# Mystical Tools for Business Success

Wouldn't it be great to go into work every day with the confidence that you have more going for you than just your experience and knowledge? Say you had some special force working with you that helped you achieve success. That would be magickal, wouldn't it? Well, that's what *Corporate Magick* is all about. It's in your hands right now, and it's the first and only book of its kind that shows you how, by using magick (the traditional spelling, to differentiate it from stage magic) and its centuries-old arcane tools, you can actually influence reality. And don't be put off thinking that you'll have to study for hours or wear a wizard's hat. Even if you're not interested in the background of why and how magick works, *Corporate Magick* works nonetheless because the entire system is based on applying magickal principles to actual business scenarios, without years of study, endless rituals, and confusing incantations.

*Corporate Magick* is a unique and radical departure from the thousands of other "occult" manuals available today. Although they all serve a purpose, this book's geared toward business success without being bogged down in magickal detail. I'm not attempting to deliver a historical or authoritative study on the occult. There are numerous books that do a wonderful job that you can find at your bookstore (see Appendix: Resources). *Corporate Magick* is a handbook for using magickal technique for business. Orthodox sorcerers and famed occultists will probably look down their noses at such a "bastardization" of age-old wisdom. But it's time that magick be applied to the real world in order to accomplish *real* results in the most important arena in the world—your livelihood.

## Why Magick Works in Business

You're probably asking yourself how two seemingly different disciplines—business and magick—become intertwined. More importantly, how do practicing corporate magicians (yes, they are out there) work their wonders without fear of being labeled crackpots or, worse, witches or devil worshipers? They work together because business and magick blend on the plane of existence we call "success." They're both disciplines that are conducted as a means to an end. And when the corporate magician applies his faith and skills, the money flows.

Most magick disciplines are well-honed crafts. And crafts are methods of creating something tangible. The tools of magick are spells, talismans (charms and objects), potions, rituals, and ceremonies. They are all used to achieve a desired result. For example, witchcraft has spells for obtaining money, voodoo can help ward off a rival or nemesis, and astrology can aid in predicting the future. Magick has always been used for gain, so with some fine-tuning, *Corporate Magick* borrows from each discipline and makes the magick work in the realm we call the business world. Witchcraft spells can get you that raise, voodoo can aid in getting you that promotion over a competitor, and astrology can help you pick stocks.

And what's equally important is that there's nothing inherently evil or unethical about using these special powers. People are often frightened by what they don't understand, and most simply don't know what magick's all about. If magick is used for personal good and gain, without direct harm to anyone else, then it's perfectly fine. You may have heard of the witches' rede that states, "An it harm none, do what thou wilt." That means exactly what it says: Don't use magick malevolently and you'll be fine. What's more, most occult practitioners believe that any intentionally harmful use of magick will come back to the instigator threefold. So, let it work for you positively and enjoy its rewards.

And the rewards can be impressive. Take my former business associate Jake, for example, who is very much into his horoscope and using astrological charting. Jake used his own brand of magick to successfully play the stock market.

Although I was always interested in the occult, I never looked at Jake's fascination with the stars as being in the same league as hard-core magick. Jake would base his stock selections on the positions of the planets (the "government," as he called them) using his own brand of magick, and more times than not he scored. He devised a plan for making money based on tried-and-true astrological methods that included the charting of the sun signs and the cycles of the moon. Jake explained to me that each of the sun signs has astrological properties and traits that affect the stock market, just as they affect people's lives.

The success of a particular stock has a lot to do with when it was "born" and its continuing life cycle, according to Jake. Each astrological sun sign has specific traits that will apply to the strength or weakness of a stock. And each sign has a corresponding "house" that also influences the sign. The sun sign's traits and its house combine and become the key indicators of how he uses his magick.

"I would first determine when a company would report its earnings—this is my barometer of its health," Jake said. "If it was during an astrological time that favored aggressive growth, I knew it was a safe bet that the company would grow. I also considered if its sun sign's house had favorable connotations. For example, company 'X' reported its earnings during June under the sign of Gemini. One of Gemini's traits is creativity, and considering that this company was in entertainment, it looked good. I bought the stock, it grew, and I made money."

The times when Jake wasn't "on the money," he chalked up the loss to an error in his calculations—not a misalignment of the stars. Jake firmly believes that the stars are never wrong. And I realized something surprising and equally astounding. It was his *faith* in winning at the stock game more than his astrological exercises that helped him achieve success. It was his *belief*—the essential key ingredient in magick—that made him money. His focused will, charged by his belief in the stars, influenced his stock choices. The bottom line is that astrology, like all magick, will work if you believe it will work.

A friend and colleague, Marcus Goodwin, author of *The Psychic Investor* (Adams Media, 2000) says that the next logical step for Wall Street is psychic investing and using oracles like tarot cards, astrology, and pendulums that can assist in predicting stock market trends and company performance. Marcus says, "I believe in the occult because I have used its tools and they have worked. Can millions of us be wrong? . . . Even J. P. Morgan, one of the world's greatest investors, hired financial astrologer Evangeline Adams to navigate his fortune—a milestone for the field of financial astrology and Wall Street alike."

So I reasoned that if playing the market with stars in your eyes (literally) could provide financial success, then using magick—the occult kind, a much more intense application—could aid in many different business disciplines and possibly grant riches to almost anyone beyond his wildest dreams.

## How Magick Works

Magick works by tapping into the unseen forces of the universe through the magician's beliefs, thoughts, and will. We're under a grand misconception that we're separate from the universe because we're individuals with bodies and minds of our own. But in reality, we are part of a much larger whole. Most magicians hold with the axiom, "As above, so below," which means that whatever is conjured and sent into the ethereal plane (the universe itself) will directly affect the earthly or physical plane. Some occultists will argue that there are different types of magick, with differing results. For example, witchcraft or Wicca works more closely with natural laws and physics, and it often shows quick, earthly results. Other more ceremonial disciplines are executed on the higher planes of the supernatural and affect the magician's spiritual nature with longer, but more effective results. But for our purposes, we will subscribe to the fact that all magickal workings tap the universe, and the actions will manifest themselves here.

And what we must continue to remember as corporate magicians is that *we are not separate from the tremendously complex universal plane.* We can directly influence what goes on around us—we just need to recognize how, and use the right tools. We are the conduits—magickal spells and items are the tools. Together we make magick.

And to further bolster your belief in magick's ability, consider *Corporate Magick*'s *simple* "zeitgeist"—*magick is science that's not yet understood.* If I told you three hundred years ago (which you will see is not that long in our evolutionary scale of magick) that you'd be able to hear and see people living their lives in a box called a "television" that sits on your table, you'd have looked at me like I was a lunatic. Or more likely, you'd try to have me burned at the stake as a witch. As trite as an analogy as it might be, some of what was thought of as magick hundreds and thousands of years ago is, in many cases, today's science. This is also how much of today's magick will be perceived in the future. Changing circumstance in accordance with your own will, telepathy, traveling the astral plane, and more will become more commonplace as magick is further researched and used for benefit.

As much of a skeptic as you may be, you cannot deny a phenomenon like déjà vu—the intense feeling of having been somewhere before or having experienced some past event. You're consciously aware of what's going to happen a split second before it occurs, and you can almost explain it as the event is unfolding. Still, you're never able to get in complete sync with the experience. Is that a yet-undiscovered scientific phenomenon, or is it magick?

Science today can't explain magick, just as science hundreds of years ago couldn't explain a solar eclipse. But these strange things are true. Many magicians claim that magick *is* magick precisely because it cannot be explained by scientific principle in the laboratory. I say we haven't yet tapped our powers, so how can we measure them? Just because we can't see them doesn't mean they don't exist. In fact, some of today's magick *will* become tomorrow's science. I believe we'll be able to command our minds to perform incredible feats of communication and healing. There has been a tremendous upsurge in the mind–body connection in health and self-improvement over the last ten years. Notable authors and lecturers such as Deepak Chopra and Dr. Wayne W. Dyer have been widely read to the acclaim of millions. And every self-help guru from Jose Silva to Norman Vincent Peale and Anthony Robbins has championed the concepts of visualization and mind control as a means to positive (read: "successful") results.

One of the most influential occultists of the twentieth century, Aleister Crowley, said, "Science enables us to take advantage of the continuity of Nature by the empirical application of certain principles whose interplay involves different orders of ideas connected with each other in a way beyond our present comprehension" (*Magick in Theory and Practice*, Theorem 11). Science? Hmmmm, could be—and it sounds like magick to me.

## Do Magick the *Corporate Magick* Way

What you'll discover here is that you won't have to study the thousands of texts, books, and secret doctrines passed down through the centuries, most of which are just rehashed interpretations of the same basic books anyway, to practice corporate magick. Furthermore, you won't have to learn the whys and wherefores of banishing rituals, the interpretation of the complicated number schemes of the Kabbalah, or which talisman means what. It's the magician's inherent power that makes rituals and talismans work, not the particular language or system (as many wizened wizards would have you believe). No matter how good a book on magick might be, it was probably culled from works previously published either using the systems described there or introducing new techniques with a traditional spin. If proponents of guardian angel magick believe an actual angel is summoned to help in a ritual and you don't, that's fine. If a Wiccan (witchcraft) practitioner calls on the methods of the "wise" and performs ceremonies using herbs, oils, and the cycles of the moon, so be it. Boil it all down and it translates to *knowing* in your body and soul that the results will occur. And they will, regardless of the methods employed.

But even if we can feel the physical benefits of the results of faith, we often don't believe the *effect* happened, because we can't quantify it with a perceivable *cause*. We are conditioned to consciously deny that anything out of the known realm of possibility could exist, much less be harnessed and used for whatever purpose we'd like. But it does, and it can—through magick. And when the businessperson gets past the roadblock of thinking that what can't tangibly be perceived with our five senses isn't real, then the floodgates of the magickal world will open.

Traditional occultists will consider *Corporate Magick*'s approach to using magick as blasphemous, claiming that successful magick can only be performed by constant repetition of ceremony and lots of hard work by the magician. I say that faith in your results, coupled with a strong will, provides results. We see it all of the time in business—those who believe beyond a shadow of a doubt that they will succeed usually do. And with the help of magick—that unseen power of the universe—awesome results can be ours. Once this happens and we embrace the unknown as an ally we become "hex-ecutives," or master sorcerers in the business world.

## White Versus Black Magick

A question often posed by the would-be magician is, what's the difference between white magick and black magick? Well, some would say there's no distinction at all—magick is just magick, because what is evil to one person isn't necessary evil to another. However, most occultists agree that using magick in excess and intentionally for destruction or to harm another person *is* black magick. Those who work black magick and claim that they work it for destructive purposes are commonly called followers of the "left-hand path."

The "good-guy" sorcerers, or followers of the "right-hand path," claim to use their magick for creative and constructive purposes. They are very aware and respectful of the immutable universal law that guarantees harsh payback for our actions, both good and bad. So when white magick is performed, it is done for the benefit not only of the magician but for the world around him as well.

The dubious distinction, however, blurs in the business world—the realm of personal gain and success—where the rules are often dog-eat-dog. Because the *Corporate Magick* system was created specifically for business, we believe it's okay to use magick for success because it is a constructive and creative goal—we want better lives. And if we use magick in any sort of negative way, it's only to defend ourselves against harm. So the bottom line is to forget the black–white dilemma and do what's best for your well-being.

## How to Make Magick—Three Basic Steps

So how do we make magick? All magickal workings require certain steps to be taken, but the traditional complexity and vast amount of subtle nuances of most magickal disciplines can fill volumes. As you continue through this book, you'll learn the basic differences between ceremonial and ritual magick, and what white and black magick really mean. But for starters, what we are doing in *Corporate Magick* is identifying the methods that are essential to all magick. Here are the three basic steps that will get you started on your magickal path:

1. Believe in magick as you would in any faith system.
2. See the desired results in your mind before, during, and after a working.
3. Conduct your spells and workings as seriously as any important business task.

By following these three guidelines—which have been used by occultists through the centuries—you can perform all of the tasks that you'll find in this book, from casting spells to traveling the astral plane (have your mind travel to another place while your body remains) to making candles, amulets, and talismans.

## Reaffirm Your Beliefs

In addition to these simple instructions, the magician must not only prepare for the ritual or ceremony at hand, but also maintain a magickal frame of mind to cement his beliefs. By using strong, repetitive affirmations, the connection to the universe is constantly reinforced and the magick becomes real. Here are six statements you need to recall in your mind or say aloud. It is essential that you recite these statements before and after all of your magickal workings and spells. Don't worry if your skeptical mind doesn't buy into what each statement professes just yet. Say them anyway, and in a short time you will see the results of your magickal working . . . and you *will* believe.

### The Six Statements

1. Magick has worked for thousands of years.
2. Magick is the hidden means to success.
3. Magick can change reality.

4. Faith and will combine to create magick.
5. Thoughts are magickal tools.
6. Magick works because I *believe* it works.

By committing these six very simple yet powerfully important statements to memory, you have taken the first steps on your path to becoming a corporate magician. You must say them aloud to yourself every day, preferably when rising and before retiring. The more you repeat and believe in the power of these magickal words, the stronger your magickal prowess will become. This is not merely hyperbole tossed out to make you feel like some stage magician. It has been proven throughout the centuries that repetition of the spoken word (in prayer, ceremony, and so forth) reaffirms people's beliefs so acutely that the recitations themselves have often been attributed with actual healing. You have no doubt heard the phrase "self-fulfilling prophecy": If a person's strong belief is expressed verbally time and time again, he reaches a point where he *makes his belief happen.* The change in reality occurs because all of the magician's energies are focused on one directive and enforced by the verbal affirmation. Say it enough times and it becomes true.

In addition to expressing these six statements aloud, the magician should recite them as many times a day as can be recalled. This sets and keeps the subconscious mind working on the basic principles of magick and solidifies the belief system. I can't impress upon you strongly enough how crucial it is to *believe* what you are stating. And this simple exercise is your pathway to myriad magickal wonders that are experienced only by "those who know."

The six statements and the three basic steps are the apprentice's first set of tools. This is the primer for *Corporate Magick*. It is the basis for everything you will learn henceforth.

# CORPORATE
# MAGICK

# CHAPTER 1

# The Ivy League of Magick

In business, it's universities and temples of higher learning like Harvard and the Wharton School of Business where many corporate chieftains get their smarts. In the world of magick, the halls of academia turn down more shadowy paths that include witchcraft, Santeria, voodoo, astrology, Kabbalah, and a number of other esoteric disciplines.

Because each practice can be a religion unto itself, they each contain endless ceremonies, rituals, tools, articles, and icons that can be daunting to the goal-oriented professional. *Corporate Magick* uses the most practical and pragmatic parts of each of these "mystery schools," particularly the disciplines that directly apply to career success and financial gain. I've drawn from the basic foundations of all of these schools to create *Corporate Magick*. Each one offers help and knowledge that—when combined with your own brand of faith and will—can benefit you directly in many business endeavors, regardless of their complexity and the seeming impossibility of a task.

What follows are brief descriptions of each of my favorite magickal paths. This background will help you to understand why these particular disciplines were chosen and especially why they are germane to business and your career success. Some may criticize *Corporate Magick* for "bastardizing" traditional magickal schools simply for material gain, but we're not concerned with the self-righteous. *No one* would be using magick if it weren't for some benefit—in most cases his own. So we put the hypocrisy behind and use the universal magickal tools available to us so we can lead better lives. If you'd like to study a discipline more deeply than is described in *Corporate Magick*, check the Appendix: Resources and Bibliography for more comprehensive resources.

## Witchcraft

First off, there's nothing really scary about witchcraft, more commonly known today as Wicca or simply, the craft. Wicca is a neo-Pagan nature-based set of beliefs (or religion) that worships the duality of nature represented by a goddess and a god. It's not inherently evil or malevolent, and witches aren't monsters. In fact you've probably met a lot more scary people in the course of business than you'd meet at a witches' coven. If anything at all about witchcraft or magick is evil, it must originate with the person (the magician) who's performing the workings, not with the magickal art. The truth of the matter is that witches for the most part are everyday people who live by a cardinal rule called the witches' rede: "An it harm none, do what thou wilt." Their methods of using magick center more on the use of natural herbs and the changing seasons than any "bat's blood" and "eye of newt."

What's more, the most common greeting in witchcraft is "blessed be,"—a catchall phrase for a wish of good fortune from the gods and the universe. So any frightening assumptions you may have about witchcraft should really be laid to rest.

## CASE STUDY
## NPR's RESIDENT WITCH

Margot Adler, one of the best-known contemporary witches and author of *Drawing Down the Moon* (Penguin/Arkana Books, 1979, 1986), a comprehensive study of historical and orthodox Paganism and witchcraft, is an exemplary model of a "real" witch. As a de facto corporate magician, Adler used her own brand of magick in her chosen career as a producer for National Public Radio (NPR) and is living proof that "normal" everyday people use magick—and many use it for business gain.

A writer, as well as a radio personality, Margot always had an affinity for the goddess Athena, a deity whom she says often helps creative individuals and one whom she has invoked since she was twelve years old. As most witches will do, she called on her favorite goddess to help her in her time of need as she prepared to negotiate a new contract at the radio station some years ago. Witchcraft relies heavily on drawing from the powers of nature, and the goddess Athena is legendary for her natural strength, clarity, and power—all assets Margot knew she would need in negotiating this tough salary issue with a prior associate.

Margot was sorely aware that this person knew all the tricks of salary negotiation, so she had to resort to some power of her own. Twenty minutes before the most important telephone interview of her life, she decided to put a simple affirmation vigil in motion by calling on Athena and writing the deity's name repeatedly on a desk blotter. Magickal affirmations reinforce beliefs by reciting and repeating magickal incantations and names, so she said she visualized Athena's powers entering her as she waited for the boss to call, all the while emphasizing the goddess's spirit of humor and generosity. "I managed to release all of my fear and confusion by practicing this affirmation. I was confident that the magick would work and within twenty minutes after I made the call to the boss, I knew I would get what I wanted," Margot said.

Although there were no lightning bolts or gusts of wind blasting through her office, Margot's personal goddess answered her call, and the magick was tapped. The telephone interview proved as intense as Adler expected, often swinging both in and out of her favor. But each time she felt some doubt, she would be reminded of Athena's strength, and it flowed through her body. She could feel her strength and confidence surge; each time any negative feeling entered her mind, a light of power illuminated her thoughts, and she knew that her magick was at her side. After what felt like hours of negotiation and just when she thought she was at a loss for words or cornered into an uncomfortable position, the magick kicked in full force and she was able to make her demands in an articulate and confident manner—much to the amazement of her adversary.

Margot got the raise, and although she didn't get everything she demanded, she received more material benefits than she'd ever expected. That night at home, she immediately thanked the goddess in a celebratory ritual within the traditional circle. Margot writes in *Drawing Down the Moon*, "The circle is the declaration of sacred ground. It is a place set apart, although its material location may be a living room or a backyard. But in the mind the circle, reinforced by the actions of casting it and purifying it, becomes a sacred space 'between the worlds' where contact with archetypal reality, with the deep places of the mind—with gods if you will—becomes possible." Margot's circle contained offertory candle burning and personal affirmations attesting to the power of witchcraft, and once again cementing her belief in her mystical ally.

Another time Margot called on magick to do her business bidding was some twenty years ago, when she was being considered for a very competitive Harvard University fellowship. She again called on Athena's power using more affirmations and special magickal items including customized candles and charms. This fellowship was so important to her that she prepared well in advance, spending a lot of time connecting with her "higher self" and doing intensive affirmations that focused on her abilities. After some intense magickal workings, she landed the prestigious grant.

Despite her strong credentials and hard work preparing for the jobs, in both cases, Margot was sure to call on the magick of the craft and the goddess Athena for help, a practice she feels made the crucial difference in her career and her success.

---

Because witchcraft has been so influential in Western occult circles and because most workings in witchcraft are based on "low" magick (magick used as a means to an end, as opposed to ceremonial or "high" magick, which develop the magician's spiritual power), *Corporate Magick* borrows much of its spells and magickal approaches from this discipline.

Witchcraft, the "religion of the wise" or "old religion," predates most modern Western religions by hundreds of years, with its roots based primarily in ancient folk magick that used the stuff of nature—herbs, plants, oils, and so forth—to heal and to perform ceremonies. Early practitioners of the craft also celebrated the seasons of the year as positive representations of life that could influence their spells and workings. These special celebrations were the precursors of witches' seasonal festivals or what have come to be known as sabbats (smaller impromptu meetings are often referred to as "esbats"). Nature was further deified as the mother of nature or goddess—the female bringer of life. Depending on the particular sect or coven, the central goddess is referred to as Diana, Gaea, Demeter, Astarte, Athena, Kore, and many other names.

The strong association with women is also carried over in witchcraft's celebration of the three stages of life referred to as the Maiden (youth), the Mother (middle age), and the Crone (also Hag or Wise One—senior years). The last one is probably why general society typically associates witches with old, crooked-nosed, broom-flying hags, instead of the incredibly diverse, creative, and intriguing group of Pagans they truly are.

The triple aspects of the life cycle are also associated with the moon and its lunar cycles—the Maiden corresponds to the new or waxing moon, the Mother to the full moon, and the Crone to the waning moon. These connections to natural phenomena built a powerful belief system that is the basis for casting spells and performing the art of witchcraft.

Although most witchcraft, and especially the more modern brand of Wicca, is centered on female deities, the male figure is also revered as a co-deity in most covens outside the strict female-dominated Dianic sect. The most popular discipline of this kind is Gardnerian witchcraft, started in the mid-1950s by Gerald B. Gardner in England. This sect proposes that not only the goddess, but her male consort, play equally important roles.

Another common following is Seax-Wica, started by Raymond Buckland. The author of many books and videos on the craft and one of the most comprehensive "how-to" witchcraft books published; *Buckland's Complete Book of Witchcraft*, Buckland points out that the duality of the deities demonstrates both feminine and masculine aspects of the same god. This can be comforting to the career-minded practitioner who needs to focus energies from either masculine or feminine viewpoints.

The male counterpart of the goddess is the horned god, most often depicted as Cernunnos from the Latin "the Horned One," or the Roman god Pan, also a horned creature. This horned male deity in witchcraft is often erroneously tied to the evil Christian devil or Satan. The fact is that the only recognized brand of organized Satanism today, the Church of Satan, founded by Anton Szandor LaVey in 1966, is anything but evil; it is made up of a diversely eclectic group of individual thinkers and creative people. Nevertheless, as I've already pointed out, witchcraft in itself is not based in evil, and today's witches vehemently oppose links with Satanism in any form. Students of the occult tend to agree that the link to real evil had its roots in Christianity's infamous fourteenth- to seventeenth-century witch hunts, where any religious practice outside of Christianity was considered the work of an evil devil.

Witchcraft's spells and workings are empowered by the goddess or god through a set of rules called the "witches' pyramid," which call for practitioners to have a "virulent imagination," a "will of fire," "rock-hard faith," and "a flair for secrecy." These tenets fit well in the world of business and make witchcraft, as you'll discover later, a valuable source for the workings of *Corporate Magick*.

## Santeria

Like many occult disciplines, Santeria, or *Regla de ocha* (the rule of the *orisha*), contains abundant symbolism and ritual, and, in fact, the term "Santeria" itself refers to the worship of Roman

Catholic–inspired saints because of its Afro-Caribbean history of Christian influence and forced acceptance. Although the magick of Santeria involves a good deal of sacrifice—including animals and other "gifts to the gods"—it lends itself well to *Corporate Magick* because it petitions a diverse pantheon of gods or *orishas,* who grant gifts of power, wealth, and revenge. Centered in Cuba, Puerto Rico, and Brazil (called *Macumba*), Santeria has roots in the gods of the African Yoruba tribes. The most important of the *orishas* are the Seven African Powers—Elleggua, Obatala, Chango, Oggun, Orunla, Yemaya, and Oshun—each of whom represents a particular human quality and is summoned to perform certain tasks.

Because of its strong association with Catholic saints, Santeria is looked upon mostly as a "white magick" or a constructive discipline, which is comforting to those concerned over dabbling in the "dark arts." However, Santeria magicians, known as *santeros* (male) and *santeras* (female), can also perform spells that do harm as well as good. Applying these types of spells can come in handy in business when defending yourself against a career-threatening nemesis or an obstinate business partner.

As I've pointed out, most Santeria spells are conducted by making offerings to the gods in the form of animal sacrifice, a much-maligned and controversial practice. Practitioners justify the rituals, however, by claiming that the animals are killed in a humane manner and then eaten, pointing out that animals are slaughtered and eaten regularly in most civilized countries. Although these powerful sacrifices to the *orishas* regularly involve animals and bloodletting, we will focus on other offerings for *Corporate Magick* purposes, and when necessary, use a liquid potion known as dragon's blood that can be substituted and will be more than sufficient. Dragon's blood can be found in most occult stores and particularly in Hispanic-community religious stores called *botanicas.*

---

## CASE STUDY
## TAKING STOCK IN SANTERIA

---

A business associate of mine, James, a Wall Street trader, has dabbled in magick since his childhood. His family is of Cuban heritage, and he tells me they are heavily involved in Santeria, often offering gifts to the *orishas,* the various saints and deities of Santeria. He says that by giving something that fits a deity's particular power, James expects that he will be granted a favor or protection. He has often told me how he experiences stock "tips" from the unknown that he can't explain. He says it's just a hunch sometimes, but whenever he consciously offers the customary bread roll soaked in milk and honey to Oshun, a prosperity deity, he never fails to receive some good news in return. "I prepare the roll, insert a yellow candle in a small hole, light it, and the money just seems to pour in," James claims. He explains that he understands the principles of the magickal workings in his offerings, but because he's so grounded in the reality of the corporate world he admits sometimes it's hard to believe the rituals work. "But then I see the results, and that's good enough for me. They work just about every time as long as I visualize the positive outcome."

---

Food plays an especially important role in the nonceremonial aspects of Santeria because of its life-giving qualities and also because it was considered a more benign ingredient to use than sacrificed animals or blood. As you'll discover in a later chapter, the offering of sweets to one creative director's personal deity helped her advertising job flourish.

Along with the use of food offerings and potions, Santeria rituals involve hypnotic drum beating that is used to invoke the *orishas,* traditionally during special feasts celebrated in the honor of a Catholic saint. Through a ritual dance, the *santero* is possessed by the spirit of the *orisha,* which replaces the practitioner's personality. The *santero* is then capable of communicating with the god and expressing his needs and intentions.

A corporate magician may not invite a spirit to enter into him, but the method of using the Santeria dance rituals for "psyching" himself into the proper frame of mind to cast a spell is a powerful catalyst. You'll learn later how drums set the stage for a Santeria ritual aimed at financial success.

## Voodoo

A first cousin to Santeria also based heavily on African folklore and magick is voodoo (sometimes referred to as "Voudon")— which literally translates into "introspection into the unknown," or "spirit," depending on the language translated. Primarily an amalgamation of slave religions and ancestral customs more than a magickal practice, it is estimated that over sixty million people practice voodoo in various countries, including Haiti, the Dominican Republic, Benin, and the United States. When most people think of voodoo, they think of wax or cloth dolls fashioned into human likenesses and pierced with pins to exact revenge. And although serious practitioners regard this as Hollywood mumbo jumbo, it is an effective brand of sympathetic and symbolic magick that we use for our own practical purposes in *Corporate Magick*. As with all magick, inanimate objects are empowered with a universal energy—in the case of voodoo, the *loas* or spirit gods, are called upon to "juice" talismans, potions, magick bags, or what have you.

But it is also wise to understand some of the history and other practices of voodoo that are the foundation of this very powerful magickal system, because this understanding will better prepare you to strengthen your faith in its workings.

Voodoo is an esoteric blend of gods, sun, and serpent worship and, surprisingly, like Santeria, borrows from Roman Catholic ceremony. It is even influenced by the legends of Moses. Pictures of Catholic saints were adopted as "front men" to camouflage the representations of voodoo gods during the time Christian colonists tried to suppress folk religions in seventeenth-century Haiti. And Moses' influence can be seen in the name of the major voodoo god Danbhala Wedo Ye-H-we—similar to "Yahweh," the name for the Hebrew God of the Old Testament.

The major voodoo gods, called *mysteres* or *loas,* are thought to be departed people who lived exemplary lives, much like Christian saints. These gods and "invisibles" are called upon to aid in magick, but their job is mostly for healing and to answer prayers of need. In most cases, voodoo priests only use magick for gain when it is for protection, and even then they consider it to be "black magick." Then again, I suppose there weren't many hostile corporate takeovers in seventeenth-century Haiti that would influence voodoo practitioners otherwise.

Connecting with the other world, particularly the dead, is a core theme in voodoo. Members of the religion believe that all people have souls with two distinct parts—a *gros bon ange* or "big guardian angel," and a *ti bon ange,* or "little guardian angel"— that pass on to different places at death, but both can also assist in a wide range of earthly scenarios after their departure. This probably accounts for the zombie myths in horror movies and novels. Although some hallucinogenic concoctions prepared in voodoo ceremonies can create a "zombielike" state in some individuals, real zombies for the most part are the stuff of superstition. Some office supervisors, however, would disagree concerning some of their employees.

Also central to this magick discipline is a wider pantheon of gods of which the primary deity is the sun god Papa Legba, the CEO of voodoo, who is the liaison to all other voodoo spirits. In fact, most voodoo practice generally revolves around the solar influence. In voodoo, temples of worship, a pillar within the physical structure—a *potomitan*—aligns with the sun, and offerings are made at its base.

A popular element of voodoo is the mojo or *gris-gris* (pronounced gree-gree) bag, a magickal tool that can induce positive or negative magick. It is usually a cloth or leather pouch with a drawstring that contains potions, trinkets, and charms—and sometimes herbs or human fingernail clippings and hair—for use in spells and for protection. *Corporate Magick*'s answer to the *mojo* bag will most likely ride along in a briefcase or portfolio—

anything the businessperson carries to and from work. The *mojo* bag is the voodoo practitioner's most personal possession. And because so many magickal items are placed in one small area, the *mojo* bag is a container of concentrated power that must be protected and kept secret from the world at large.

## CASE STUDY
## THE MAGICKAL TRADER

A successful Boston stock trader featured in the *Wall Street Journal* got his *mojo* working by becoming as famous for his use of voodoo dolls and magick amulets as he is for his business acumen.

Brokers are traditionally a superstitious lot, using expensive pens to take orders hoping "like" will attract "like," and of course never using a red pen (red denoting financial loss). But Mike offered more to the "trading gods" than respect for superstition. Having dabbled in esoteric arts for years, Mike convinced his coworkers to create a small cloth voodoolike poppet doll that would act as a spiritual medium to rescue declining stocks. Mike knew from experience that a poppet used with the right rituals could affect people's lives, so (he reasoned) why not use a poppet to swing a downward financial trend back to a positive position?

The traders began daily rituals that included listing the plummeting stocks on a scrap of paper and attaching it to the doll. Mike and his newfound stock sorcerers jabbed a white head pin into the sagging symbols while mentally concentrating on turning the stocks around. And although there were no apparent "supernatural phenomena" as this mysterious business cabal performed its rituals, in many cases the weak stocks rebounded. Needless to say, the ragged poppet became a regular magickal addition to Mike's trading desk and a constant reminder to the suit-and-tie crowd of the power of the magick they supplied.

But if by some chance the voodoo doll failed, Mike resorted to an amulet made by his children that he calls his "Amulet of Courage." The simple but effective charm, made from a clove of garlic wrapped in purple silk with a long cord, resides in Mike's desk just in case of magickal emergencies. He feels that although the charm has no traditional magick preparation, it is infused with his children's pure love and is very powerful in its own right. "They read a book on magick and put this charm together," Mike said. He believes that an article, any article, that has been charged with positive energy—especially by loved ones—can work wonders. His belief in this kind of business magick became the charm to facilitate his goals.

And it wasn't long before the clove was put to the test. One evening, after dealing a bad four-hundred-million-dollar trade, Mike turned to the amulet for help. In the glow of a full moon he focused all of his will, clutched the charm in his hands, and asked the universal powers to clean up the mess.

By the next day he'd managed to recover thirty million. Not a complete victory, but nevertheless a minor miracle by Wall Street standards.

---

# The Kabbalah

The hidden wisdom of Jewish occult doctrine is the Kabbalah (spelled many ways—Kabala, Cabala, Qabala, among others), a complicated magickal system of numbers, planets, and a treelike diagram that represents God, man, and the universe and includes a complex set of instructions for the magician on how to tap into its powers.

Called *hokmah nistarah,* the "hidden wisdom," the Kabbalah's roots are based firmly in Judaism. However, another form, sometimes called Hermetic Kabbalah, influenced by an eclectic mix of Gnostic, Egyptian, Christian, Rosicrucian, and Freemasonic rituals, is closer to what most people think of and practice as the Kabbalah today.

Although the Kabbalah is difficult to master even for the most astute sorcerer, it is an important aspect of any form of magick. Most master rituals are based on Kabbalah principles, including the most famous—the Banishing Ritual of the Lesser Pentagram—a universal high magick ceremony used to accomplish magickal goals and invoke spirits. *Corporate Magick* magicians won't have to be concerned with the grueling detail required in these rituals; suffice it to say that they form the basic instructions for most higher magickal ceremony and are most valuable to scholarly magickal pursuits. Certain core principles will be adapted, however. For example, pure concentration and imagination—essential ingredients to Kabbalah rituals—are important tools to the corporate magician. Keep in mind that the *Corporate Magick* system extracts only what will provide the magician with practical power by focusing on the Kabbalah's methods of achieving material success. However, knowing its history will make using it clearer to the business magician.

Believed to have been developed in the time of Abraham, the Jewish patriarch of the Old Testament, the Kabbalah has influenced many magicians and magickal systems since the fifteenth century, including the nineteenth-century magician Eliphas Levi (real name Alphonse Louis Constant). Levi was an accomplished leader in the magickal society of the Golden Dawn and was the author of classic magickal texts *Transcendental Magic* and, later, *The Keys to the Mysteries,* which revealed many of the perceived secrets of the Kabbalah. Levi's interpretation of the Kabbalah contributed much to the modern Hermetic Kabbalah.

Aleister Crowley, a later luminary of the magickal society the Golden Dawn and one of the most famous magicians of the twentieth century (who himself believed he was the reincarnation of Levi and was the self-proclaimed "Beast 666"), was also influenced by the Kabbalah. In fact, Crowley diagramed a detailed, albeit more hedonistic, look at the basis of the Kabbalah, the Tree of Life, in his book *777.*

The Kabbalah's Tree of Life is a diagram of ten spheres called the Sephiroth (emanations from God) that are connected by twenty-two lines representing the letters of the Hebrew alphabet (see figure 1, overleaf). This interconnection, called the Path of Wisdom, combines to show a miniature link between the universe, God, and man. Each sphere of the Sephiroth represents an aspect of God and man and has a particular goal associated with it, such as victory, love, wealth, and others. These tangible goals work particularly well with *Corporate Magick*'s "results-oriented" system. It will be these spheres we work with closely in chapter 8 when we get into the use of the Kabbalah.

The spheres of the Sephiroth, called "Splendid Lights," are guarded by preassigned archangels (Raphael, Michael, Gabriel, or Uriel) as well as by groups of lesser angels who are summoned for assistance in Kabbalah ceremonies. The spheres also correspond to colors, planets, virtues, vices, herbs, foliage, gems, animals, and magickal symbols, and are divided into three columns or pillars on the Tree of Life glyph. The right-hand pillar represents the male active/positive path; the left, the female or passive/negative path; and the middle path, which represents harmony and mildness, contains both male and female attributes.

By magickal manipulation of the spheres through evocations and conjuring, the magician draws down the cosmic lightning with which God was said to create the universe. This is important to *Corporate Magick* because this aspect of magickal working of the Kabbalah is the primary method to be used for material gain. The magician absorbs this cosmic light and gains the power to achieve what he needs.

The most important sphere or Sephira that will concern us is Malkuth, which represents the kingdom of the material world as well as the magician himself. Malkuth contains the most tangible energy of the tree, and by tapping into it, the magician harnesses the power to perform magickal tasks in the material world.

Numbers also play an essential role in the workings of the Kabbalah in a discipline called *gematria*. In most cases, this approach fits well into the *Corporate Magick* system by virtue of the business world's "bottom-line" thinking. For example, if money is desired, the word "money" must be broken down into its five-letter value. The sum of these five letters then corresponds to a Hebrew letter that has a special Kabbalah numerical value (its secret power). That number is influenced by a state of consciousness controlled by one of the ten spheres. So once the numerical value is discovered, the magician locates the sphere of consciousness that can control the desired result and then works his magick through that sphere—summoning the power of God. However,

## FIG. 1 The Spheres and the
## Tree of Life

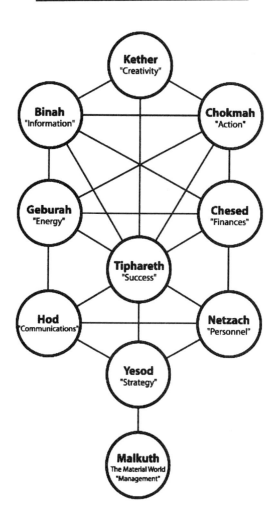

because the letter and number combinations would require a computer to decipher, I felt it better left for future study if you're so inclined.

The Kabbalah's Tree of Life also uses color to influence workings. For instance, if the magician is seeking material goods by working with the sphere of Malkuth, which is black in color, then he should surround himself with black candles.

Despite its elaborate system and often-confusing approach to achieving simple results, the Kabbalah is the basis for much of the Western occult world's esoteric teachings. So it was from here where we mined the system for *Corporate Magick* "gems." And although the paths to obtaining results seem at first daunting and complex because of the Kabbalah's intricate workings, the system is genuinely results-oriented on both a spiritual and material plane. Results are what we're after, after all, and like the business world itself, hard work usually pays off.

---

## CASE STUDY
### MAGICKAL PROPERTIES

---

Even the rich and famous have embraced the Kabbalah, including TV and movie star Roseanne Barr, comedian Sandra Bernhard, and even Madonna, who has a song about the Kabbalah on her *Ray of Light* CD.

Roseanne's public endorsement of the practice was so convincing that it prompted Phyllis, a commercial real estate broker in Los Angeles, to use the system so she might score some major deals. Phyllis was always fascinated with New Age practices and, being of Jewish ancestry, she often heard talk about the mysteries of the Kabbalah at family gatherings—despite it being considered by some to be taboo magick. However, she reasoned that there must be something beneficial to the workings if some people were afraid of them and others sung their praise.

After attending some local seminars at colleges and New Age shops, interviewing teachers of the art, and getting a solid foundation of knowledge, Phyllis was ready to put the practice to work. It was a slow period for commercial real estate in her area of the San Fernando Valley back in the mid-1990s, so she decided on a lark to try her hand at the ancient system in an effort to drum up business.

Working with the Kabbalah's Tree of Life, a magician identifies and uses the power of the divine for personal gain. Although most students of the mystery schools find that successfully using the Kabbalah is extremely complicated and requires many years of study, Phyllis intuitively felt closeness with the Kabbalah and used its basic principles in her ceremonies.

"I knew that by locating the right sphere [a circle on the chart diagram] on the Tree of Life that represented what I needed, I could perform a ceremony that would work to my advantage," she said. "My studies showed me that by manipulating the number system and invoking the correct combinations of spheres on the tree, my wishes could come true. I experimented at first with small gains, like finding bargains at stores I planned to shop. And most times, if I really applied my knowledge and my concentration on invoking the power, my expectations were met."

So when Phyllis sought bigger and better successes, she decided to work with the sphere of Malkuth, the Sephira that represented "the Kingdom." Phyllis interpreted "the Kingdom" as a metaphor for real estate, and that's where she needed help. Drawing a schematic of the Tree of Life, she emphasized the parts of the system that could benefit her with the corresponding colors and numbers as well as spheres. She lit the appropriately colored candles and concentrated her will on gaining leads that would help her business.

Within hours of the ceremony, Phyllis began to experience small changes in the direction of her business. She would walk down blocks she normally avoided and spot empty storefronts. She met people who were looking to expand their businesses and was able to suggest larger spaces. But the most mysterious event was at a cocktail party given by a close friend at which Phyllis was introduced to a senior vice president of a large firm that needed to relocate to Phyllis's area. If that wasn't serendipitous enough, after some lengthy conversation, she asked the V.P. for his card and was amazed to see he represented a *forestry* company—a positive development involving the Kabbalah's "Tree" of Life that in Phyllis's mind was much more than sheer coincidence.

She arranged to meet with the businessman at a later date, and after consulting the Kabbalah's Tree again, she saw that he needed an area that was not going to upset the local community's commercial–residential balance. Most agents would have tried to pitch *any* area to close such a big deal, but Phyllis knew beforehand about the V.P.'s environmental concerns. She presented him with a number of choices, and within minutes he discovered the land he needed and she made the sale. From that day forward, Phyllis never entered a real estate deal without first consulting her new business associate and consultant—the ancient Kabbalah.

# Astrology

In the last few years, especially during the millennium madness, we've heard a lot about using astrology to do everything from pick winning stocks to pinpointing Armageddon and the cataclysmic end of the world. Since the beginning of the year 2000, the occult world itself—no stranger to foretelling the future—was also besieged with futuristic astrological business predictions, from the collapse of the economy as we know it to amassing great fortunes by turning to the stars.

The truth is that some people—those who really know what astrology's all about—do follow their charts and are often successful despite popular changes in decades or years that end in "66." A magickal colleague of mine, Marcus Goodwin, author of *The Psychic Investor*, actually took a challenge to prove that astrology can affect finances. Goodwin said that he'd make a million dollars day-trading stocks by using astrology and psychic powers. Goodwin knows astrological techniques, how to read the zodiac and the positions of the planets. So he is adept at separating the "bull" from the bear—so to speak. And when he started his quest for a fortune using astrology, his system literally began to pay off! Starting with twenty-five hundred dollars, Goodwin nearly doubled his money after only a month of trading. By using his knowledge of the stars, coupled with his intuitive psychic powers, he claims he will double the gains nine times in less than a year for more than one million dollars.

Using astrology for wealth and success requires that we tap into the planetary happenings all around us that have been studied since Babylonian times—around 3000 B.C., or perhaps even before that. The Greeks, ancient Indians, the Mayans, and the Chinese all used forms of astrology to predict the future and to discover signs of imminent disaster or prosperity. At the core of all of astrology is the common magickal phrase, "As above, so below," a phrase you'll hear repeatedly in this book. In other words, all events in the cosmos affect what happens on earth, whether it is by magickal invocation or using the stars as cosmic guideposts.

There are essentially two branches of astrology that we will deal with in *Corporate Magick*—natal astrology, which directly affects a person, and mundane astrology that deals with nations and large groups of people. Because both of these areas can affect your success, analysis of astrological charts should be done for both. Your chart might reflect a prosperous day, but unless you know in which part of the world your stock is performing, your investments could be in jeopardy.

Astrology centers on the zodiac, a circle of beings and symbols with twelve different sun signs that are familiar to most people from their daily newspaper horoscopes. They are: Aries, Taurus, Gemini, Cancer, Leo, Virgo, Libra, Scorpio, Sagittarius, Capricorn, Aquarius, and Pisces. Each one of these signs is ruled by a planet named for a mythological god, including Venus, Mars, Mercury, Jupiter, Saturn, Uranus, Neptune, and Pluto as well as the sun and the moon. Although most people believe that the planets influence them because of who the deity is (that is, if Mars is the god of war, then Mars signifies turmoil), most astrologers conversely believe the planets were named because of how they affected life, and not vice versa.

The twelve signs are also related to the four elements: earth (Virgo, Taurus, Capricorn), air (Gemini, Libra, Aquarius), fire (Aries, Leo, Sagittarius), and water (Cancer, Scorpio, Pisces), referred to as "quadrupities" and "triplicities." In addition, there are five major planetary aspects or influences that astrologers must take into consideration. They are conjunction, which can be positive or negative; opposition and square, which are negative; and trine and sextile, which are both positive.

All of these pieces are then charted on a horoscope or zodiac map that takes into consideration the most crucial part of astrology—time of birth (exact time is often "fudged" in something called rectification that allows for a number of different birth times). So think of the zodiac as an imaginary canvas dividing the sky, with the date of a person's birth at the center. This division of twelve parts is the "houses," and each house has its "Department of Life" with its particular attributes. For example, the second house deals with money and possessions, and the tenth house has to do with career—two houses that will become important to the corporate magician.

Special tables called "Ephemerides" locate the positions of signs and planets on the eastern horizon at the time and place of birth. The point where your eastern horizon intersected your sign on the zodiac is called the "ascendant," an important part of the charting process. So corporate magicians with their signs and ruling planet ascending in the second or tenth houses would most likely be in an advantageous position for business success.

By charting individuals, companies, bosses, coworkers, and so on, the corporate magician will be able to "map out" a concise plan to help achieve his goals.

Astrology, as well as all of the magickal disciplines briefly introduced here, will be honed for your business success in the chapters that follow. We take the most essential elements of each mystery school and give it the *Corporate Magick* spin so you can begin working with magick that can help your career and your livelihood. The advantage of the *Corporate Magick* system is that you can use it right away. All it takes is for you to discover the magickal path that appeals to you most, whether it be witchcraft, astrology, voodoo, or the Kabbalah. Then, combine the easy steps along with a lot of faith in these tried-and-true methods and you can become a master sorcerer in the hallowed halls of Wall Street or in your very own small business.

# CHAPTER 2

# Preparing the Magician

Preparing yourself to do magick in business is all about psyching yourself up for the task at hand, just as you would do in any work situation where you know you need to be at your best. But in magick, you're not going to recite what you'll say to the boss or the bank executive. Your recitations will be affirmations, rhymes, incantations, and whatever other verbal method you'll create for yourself to focus your will to a laser-sharp tool. You're going to transform yourself into a magickal chief executive—a manager of mystical abilities and supervisor of the "supernatural."

And a nice fringe benefit of working magick is that you won't be that concerned with what you should wear to the meeting or whether your statistics are on the money. Because you'll be working on a different plane of reality—the ethereal plane, or the world where you'll tap into the universe's strengths—you're going to prepare with different and, admittedly, what may sometimes feel like strange methods.

The key to your performance and preparation is to develop your senses to the point at which they will serve you better than you could ever imagine. I already introduced the three basic steps and the six statements that you must remember before performing any magick. Those affirmations are designed to get you in the right frame of mind and should be practiced daily or at least at convenient times. What follows later in this chapter are the "magick muscle-building exercises," which will actually put your magick into motion.

I'm sure you've often heard about the "sixth sense" or the "third eye"—those elusive senses that allow us to foretell the future or perform amazing feats. Psychics claim that it's this very power that allows them to see into people's futures. The sixth sense has been attributed to many amazing feats, from predicting disasters to picking winning lottery numbers. But the "seers" and "sages" who claim dominion over the "gift," as it's also sometimes referred to, in most cases will not explain how they've come upon the power. They might say they were born with the ability, or that they're the seventh son of the seventh son, so the talent has been passed down mystically through the ages.

Well, what if I told you that *you* already possess that power? That's right, you—the would-be magician who never possessed anything mystical in your life, much less an awesome power like a sixth sense that will allow you to perform miracles. And what's more, you use this gift all the time. You just don't know it. As a corporate magician you're going to hone that sense so well that it will make your magick astoundingly successful.

That being said, the fact is, there is no sixth sense—not one that's measurable by contemporary standards or empirical study anyway. This hidden sense is actually the culmination of all of the other senses coordinated and orchestrated by your very own mind. And it can be developed, like a muscle, by using the subconscious power of the mind—the magician within.

Think back to old cowboy movies in which the Indians were able to "hear" the hoofbeats of enemy horses miles away. And you may have heard of Aboriginal tribesman who can "smell" water in the ground. Both feats of amazing ability, and both based on *absolute concentration*. The Indian's and the Aborigine's focus were so acute that they were able to control their other five senses in a method that worked miracles. Focusing, or becoming keenly aware of what's around you at the very instant you are concentrating, is the first step.

Try this right now: Look at this printed word on the page:

## MESMERIZE.

Notice its color, its shape, and its size. Now look at the paper itself; feel its texture. See how the letters sit on the page and become three dimensional as you stare at them, almost floating. Although all of that sensory input was always present, you only became completely aware when you consciously became focused. You've instantly become much more aware of the shapes, sizes, and textures of the printed word and page and their interplay with each other simply by focusing your mind. This is a constant occurrence—your brain works by allowing you to focus on one task at a time so you can function, but your *mind,* your inner magician, is capable of much, much more.

There's nothing new about mind control, focused concentration, visualization, or similar concepts. There have been enough mind-power schools and self-help techniques developed over the past half century to fill a library. But the difference in magick, and what all master sorcerers have known for thousands of years, is that preparing yourself to work spells and enchantments requires solid technique and trancelike meditation, but it also requires a pure belief that you are tapping a higher power. Call it the universe, gods, demons, spirits, angels—whatever you feel in your heart that you truly believe is the catalyst, the coach, and the facilitator of the magick you wish to perform. It may sound like New Age hype, but trust me, putting your faith into that intangible power *will* make magickal things happen in your life. It has worked for hundreds of my fellow magicians and it can work for you.

As a corporate magician, you'll have the benefit of thousands of years of knowledge handed down from sorcerers all over the world as to how to prepare to perform your feats of wonder. The best part about the *Corporate Magick* system is that you need only concern yourself with three steps before doing any kind of spell.

Keep in mind that the three-step preparation is really geared for intense workings and spell casting. You can always use the quick spells provided in this book without going through the entire preparation process. And, of course, it's a matter of time and inclination. If you have the time to prepare, by all means go through the three steps so your magick will work to its fullest. And even if you don't have a particular spell in mind and just want to exercise your magickal muscle, that's fine too.

You must, however, complete the preparation at least one time before you try any magick. The reason for this is that it will acquaint you with the process for future magick, but more importantly, it will tune your mind to the universal force that will ultimately assist you in all of your magick. You must remember that once you become a magician, you no longer just "do" magick; you *are* magick. And from the *Corporate Magick* standpoint, preparation will open the conduit to the *Corporate Magick* Cabal of ready magicians who will then psychically recognize you later.

# The Three Steps of Preparation

## Step 1: Hone Your Sixth Sense

You are already in possession of the elusive sixth sense, so now all you need to do is wake it up. Here's an exercise that will help:

Sit in a completely darkened room with absolutely no distractions for fifteen minutes (set a timer before you turn off the lights). You may think of anything you like, but try to be in touch with your magickal mind—that is, imagine your mind having the capability of meeting, talking, and interacting with anyone who's now alive or has ever lived. Imagine that you can ask any question of that person and get expert advice. See that person in your mind's eye, talk with him, and get answers. This may feel silly at first, but think about the thousands of times you've anticipated meeting someone—anyone, be it a friend, lover, relative, or business associate. Often the meeting's similar to what you imagined it would be. You may not have known it, but you performed a bit of magick by visualizing that meeting beforehand, and what occurred in real time was influenced by your thoughts.

Once your fifteen minutes are up, immediately turn on the lights or walk out of the room into the light. Without missing a beat, pick out any object, a painting, piece of furniture, or whatever strikes you. Look at the object and dissect all of its attributes—its feel to the touch, its color, its smell; if it's food, its taste; if it makes noise, its sound. Do this for a full five minutes, then reenter the room and darken it once more.

Once back in the dark, remember all you can about the object you chose. Relive the experience and actually call on your senses to re-create the object and all its attributes. Don't just think about the object; see it with your mind. Touch it with your mind. Feel it with your mind. Taste it with your mind. Smell it with your mind. Let your mind completely take over the experience. And it will, because this is your sixth sense at work.

This tool will also train your mind to concentrate—to actually "experience with your mind." It is essential that you concentrate fully on whatever magickal spell or enchantment you launch into the universe. Even when performing simple candle magick, you must focus on the flame and direct your magick using that power of concentration. You are, in effect, enlisting objects—candles, oils, fetishes, talismans, amulets, poppets, and so on—to do your bidding, but they are only the helpers. Your mind is the master. When you concentrate and free your thoughts to travel, your wish—your magickal command—is accepted and put into action.

The second part of this exercise requires that you choose a magickal "sigil" or sign that will trigger your magickal intentions in a split second and launch your mind's wishes into the universe. For our purposes, we have supplied you with the sign of the "pentagram" (turn the page to see figure 2), a five-pointed star that's universally known in the occult community. The pentagram has many attributes and is a powerful symbol. Some believe that when it's used with its point upward, it represents the union of man and nature; pointing downward, it represents evil and chaos. It's also used in magickal disciplines to invoke or banish spirits and/or demons. We'll not concern ourselves with the theory of the pentagram; that could alone fill volumes. Suffice it to say that it has inherent magickal power, and that's why we'll use it as a point of concentration in performing *Corporate Magick*.

Performing the pentagram exercise is simple. All you need to do, in a darkened room lit only by one candle (any type will do), is to look and deeply concentrate on the diagram. Place the candle close enough to the page so the pentagram symbol can be easily seen. Now stare at the symbol for ten full minutes (use your timer again). When the time is up, blow out the candle and, while remaining in the dark, close your eyes and create a large white screen that will appear in front of your eyes. On this screen, picture the image of the pentagram that you've previously created in your mind. It is important that your eyes remain closed even if it's pitch black in your room. See with your mind how the pentagram is formed, how the lines intersect. See its size, shape, and how it sits perfectly centered on your mental screen.

Keep the pentagram's image in your mind's eye for at least another ten minutes (you can estimate), then open your eyes. You should still have the image of the pentagram visible. It should appear as though it's floating in the darkness. If you don't see the image, practice this exercise as many times a day as you can until the pentagram appears after you've opened your eyes in the dark. Once it does, you have begun to sharpen your concentration to a point where your magickal intentions can be sent into the ethereal realm. Once this technique is mastered, each time you perform a magickal spell or ritual, your focused mind will respond to your wishes almost instantaneously.

This is your ultimate entrée into the magickal realm. Your finely honed senses will work outside normal limitations, opening the portal to all magickal tasks. Despite what every occultist on the planet will preach about the correct methods in preparing for magick, the fact is that it requires a mental state receptive to the physical and ethereal planes. How you get there is your own business. But you *must* get there.

You'll find that over time, you will be much more perceptive of your immediate surroundings. You'll "pick up" on things that

**FIG. 2**

other people miss. You'll start to recognize deeper colors and more pungent smells, and you'll hear sounds previously unheard. When a thunderstorm is brewing, for example, you'll notice how the wind changes direction, how the clouds form at a rapid pace, how the air smells of the trees and grass, and you'll hear the rumble of thunder *before* most other people. In fact, you'll be able to "predict" when the thunder will start because you actually heard the rumbling miles away—much to the amazement of your associates. And this will work in any scenario because your sixth sense will be on high alert and in direct communication with the universe—your magickal ally.

The more you practice these mental exercises in which you don't just "look and see" something, but actually experience it with your mind, the sharper your overall powers of observation—your sixth sense—will be. And once it is trained to grasp everything you focus on, then it will eventually be in touch with what's unseen—the universal plane where all magick takes place.

To recap the honing of your sixth sense:

- Practice the dark/light room and object exercise whenever you have free time.
- See, feel, touch, and taste objects with your mind.
- Practice the pentagram concentration exercise and "see" it in the dark.
- Be acutely aware of your surroundings at all times—notice details.
- Firmly *believe* that your focus and concentration will open the doors for magick to work.

## Step 2: Create Your Power

Just as you might develop your career persona—your business image, so to speak—by attending certain prestigious schools, specially designed seminars or courses, or professional bodies and associations, so it will be with using *Corporate Magick*. You will need to mentally re-create yourself as a powerful business magician so that all of your desired success and power is available to you upon a moment's notice. The beauty of the *Corporate Magick* approach is that you don't have to create this persona using any bona fide institutions or governing bodies, because the image you create in the magickal world is made by any symbol of power and success of your choice, and it is created as an aid to serve only you.

In fact, it will benefit you a great deal to let your imagination and wishes go wild. Become the CEO of your dreams or the corporate raider feared in every company on Wall Street. This *is* the person you will be on the magickal plane, so there is no limit to who you might be or what you can accomplish. Remember, your willpower influences reality, so if you fancy yourself a tycoon, *be* that person in every manner, gesture, thought, idea, and goal, and the power of that person will aid you. Consider the *Corporate Magick* approach as having a Harvard MBA—and Bill Gates as your favorite uncle. *All* doors are now open to you.

A good way to establish your power is to identify with a person whom you admire in the business world, or who has reached the level of success that you desire. Many esoteric schools call on their respective gods, angels, spirits, or demons to do their magickal bidding. In *Corporate Magick,* your "spiritual guardians" should be people whom you idolize or wish to emulate in life. For example, if you idolize Donald Trump for his deal-making expertise, his wealthy lifestyle, and his playboy image, then visualize yourself as Donald Trump. Similarly, if your hero is a woman—say, Oprah Winfrey, who has made millions of dollars and is as well known as a savvy businesswoman as she is as an entertainer—then choose her as your personal "power broker." Do in your mind what she does every day—picture yourself closing huge real estate deals, opening new casinos, founding magazines, interviewing famous people, and eating at the world's finest restaurants. Once you've established who your broker is and are mentally becoming like that person, you can call on him or her to aid you in all your magickal endeavors. The shamans of ancient Native American tribes would take on the characteristics of animals they admired and worshiped out of admiration and respect, and so that the animal gods would favor them. In Santeria, the *santeros* (priests) call on Roman Catholic saints to assist in their magick. Do the same for your business heroes, calling on them before you begin a spell. Their names become powerful triggers for your magick.

Another tool in creating your personal power is tapping into the universal flow of energy. What this means is simply that the magician needs to let energy flow through his mind and body so that he strengthens his "oneness" with the universe. Earlier I pointed out that we think of ourselves as being independent bodies who live in the universe, when in fact we are *part* of the universe. Our molecules and atoms are the actual stuff of the universe. We take in oxygen, expel carbon dioxide, and constantly shed our skin and regrow. If we weren't actually a physical part of the universe, we couldn't survive. So when we say that as magicians, we must let the universal energy flow through us, it's not a far-fetched concept. What we are doing is allowing ourselves to become more efficient conduits for that energy, which then works as a tool for magick. The energy that flows carries our mental wishes into the magickal plane.

Traditional magickal theory refers to this energy as the "white light," an intense source of directed universal power. Magickal practitioners in some Far Eastern systems of yoga and in certain Kabbalah ceremonies—the Middle Pillar of Light, for example—rely heavily on this light in their ceremonies and feel that it is the very source of all goodness and the cosmic catalyst responsible for any type of magick to work. Some schools believe that the light even has the power to heal.

The light flows through the body from above the head down to the bottom of the feet, empowering the magician. As a corporate magician, you should envision this light emanating from a source that has some specific meaning to you and your goals, whether it is an anthropomorphic deity or the New York Stock Exchange. The key is to let that power energize you with a sense of confidence that allows your magick to work. Control your breathing into a rhythmic pattern, while allowing the light to stream through your body.

The method of tapping this energy flow is also simple. Before you are about to work your magick, follow these steps:

• Stand facing the east with your hands raised.
• Close your eyes and lift your head upward.

- Concentrate on your power source (person, thing, or what have you).
- Draw down the power from the source—let it enter your head and slowly filter down through your body until you feel your entire being energized.

Creating your personal power for magick is analogous to exercising your body for strength. You will feel more confident and infused with the ability to perform real magick that works. So to recap:

- Create your magickal business persona (who you want to be).
- Call on your magickal "power broker" to assist you.
- Draw down the universal energy into your mind and body.

## *Step 3: Prepare Your Chamber*

What do you feel is one of the most important benchmarks of success in the corporate world (besides a huge salary, of course)? Think about those who've "made it" and how they are rewarded for their long hours and complete dedication to the company. If you said "the corner office," then you're right in tune with most people, who value that as a premiere perk in the world of business. More important to some folks than a raise in salary or a paper promotion, the corner office (or even just a larger one) carries considerable weight throughout a company's culture. The bigger and better office says that he who inhabits this space is important, and he needs this much room to operate. And more importantly, the person who gets the cushy space with the best views and the most comfortable furniture feels more important, and more responsible than his subordinates. He's in that space because he must make things happen. He's got to get the job done. And while he's at it, his self-esteem gets a boost because he is now "master of all he surveys."

There are entire chapters in business success manuals dedicated to the "power office"—how to arrange furniture, wall plaques, and diplomas to impress, and often to intimidate. The place where you "live" in business is of paramount importance to your sense of worth. It's a measure of whether you've "arrived." What's more, the office becomes a place of familiarity and comfort—a home away from home that holds the company secrets and strategies within its file drawers. When the door is closed, do not enter. Therein lay the decisions that will rock the very foundations of the business world. It's the businessperson's temple.

And it's no different in *Corporate Magick*. The place where you will conduct your spells and ceremonies, whether elaborate or basic, has many important functions. Like the corner office, your sacred space will house your secrets and provide sanctuary away from those who may not appreciate or understand what you are doing.

Your area can be as large as a temple (an entire room) or simply a small part of a room that houses a working altar. It can be an entire grove in your backyard or just a circle drawn on the floor of your bedroom. In Wicca and other Pagan schools, this altar space can often be found in the house or outside on the magician's grounds. In most cases, an altar faces the east and is first consecrated (blessed and cleansed of malevolent spirits) with a special oil or salt water.

Pagan altars also contain items that represent the four elements—fire, water, air, and earth, and feature special magickal tools like athames (daggers), chalices, goblets, incense burners, candles, and representations of gods and deities. And there are myriad rules as to how they should be constructed and where objects are to be placed. Aleister Crowley, for example, maintained that magickal items and objects should never be mixed in with a magician's mundane possessions because their "purity" would be compromised. But *Corporate Magick* views the mundane accoutrements of business as magickal and not at all mundane because they carry the seeds of success within them. Think about that paperweight you've carried from job to job—it has become your "sorcerer's stone," your old friend, and your lucky talisman all rolled into one.

Regardless of what discipline the magician follows, all sacred spaces have one thing in common—they are physical areas where he feels he can tap into his magickal power and summon the forces that will help in his workings. This area, in effect, becomes a chamber that houses the magician's will and then acts as a catalyst to launch his wishes into the universe.

Here's what you need to do to prepare your chamber for the *Corporate Magick* ahead:

### Identify Your Space

Your chamber can be anywhere, but I recommend that you use an area that has somehow already been charged with business dealings or your personal success. My sacred space and altar are in my home office. And although I have had offices in the companies where I've worked, my home office contains many more personal and empowering items such as favorite books and photos. More importantly, it is a sanctuary of security and protection—something the often-shaky corporate world cannot offer.

So identify your space and make a point of spending time in the area undisturbed for at least an hour. It would be best to do this during the phase of the waxing new-moon to full-moon cycle. In occult lore, this is a time of renewal, liberation, and new beginnings, so it's the perfect time to create your temple of business power. It is also a prime time to visualize and speak affirmations that will be planted firmly in your subconscious (magickal) mind.

### Furnish Your Chamber

It is advisable, but not necessary, that you have an altar or at least a desktop or tabletop that can serve as a makeshift altar. You will need something that you can place objects on when performing magickal rituals, even if it's nothing more than a snack table. One of the first things you'll be required to do to ready your chamber is to pick a spot where you can safely place a candle. Don't pass over this simple but crucial step.

Furnishing your chamber can be accomplished with a few simple items—let's call them "magickal assistants"—or you can build an entire temple to the gods of commerce. It really depends on how much energy and how many positive, successful vibes you get from the items you'll live with while working your magick. Keep in mind that these objects help. But they are not mandatory. It's a matter of how much they will contribute to your overall feeling of power. The most common things found in *Corporate Magick* chambers are books—either business- and success-related volumes or biographies of captains of industry. Other items include photos and posters, diplomas, certificates of achievement, and business awards. Personal items really don't have a place here. Although they are comforting, the chamber needs to be a focused portal of *business* energy, so anything that distracts from those goals should be avoided.

My friend Allan, a Madison Avenue advertising account rep, has a room in his home where he performs his *Corporate Magick*. It contains nothing more than a chair, a desk, and a poster of David Ogilvy, a legend in the world of advertising and his industry idol. "I love my chamber," he says. "The poster of Ogilvy immediately puts me in the right frame of mind and I'm prepared for magick."

Once your chamber is outfitted with your magickal assistants, reserve some time when you're certain you won't be interrupted by people or loud noises. Sit in a comfortable chair facing the east (a magickal direction) and try to clear your mind of all thoughts except for your solitary purpose of creating this special magickal place. This is going to be your sanctum sanctorum, your holy of holies, and the area where your true magick will emerge, so your mind must first clear the way.

### Consecrate the Area

Anoint a white candle with prosperity oil, rubbing the mixture from the center upward, then downward. According to Anna Riva's book *Golden Secrets of Mystic Oils,* this oil will attract and draw luck and success in business deals. Then light your candle and concentrate on the flame, as you would do in any working. See your chamber area in your mind and feel it pulse with the power it's receiving from the business universe. Envision the masters of the business world channeling their energies into your room as it becomes alive with wisdom, knowledge, and power. Know now that you can enter this area at any time and take advantage of all the wonders it possesses.

Visualize in your mind's eye that you are closing deals, making sales, creating products, or whatever it is you want to accomplish. Feel the handshakes and hear the voices of the people you are dealing with. What you will be doing is consecrating your chamber with magickal energy that paves the way for all future workings. Some mystery schools commonly perform their magick within a nine-foot circle to protect them from demons and to focus power. Pagans traditionally consecrate sacred spaces with salt water and incense. Roman Catholics also use incense and sprinkle holy water during their masses to purify the surroundings. All these rituals prepare the space for supernatural intervention.

You also need to purify your chamber to eliminate any negative presence. I suggest that you use "high altar" incense mixes usually found at Christian supply stores. You can use any incense that appeals to you, and many occult shops have specific purification incenses that will work, but I recommend using one that is powerful yet not sweet smelling. You want the incense to do its job of "cleansing" negative energies, but you don't want it distracting you from your work at hand.

The use of salt water is particularly potent for cleansing your altar or magickal work desk. Simply wash down the area before you place any objects on it. Again, if you can perform all of these chamber preparations during the full moon, the power will be that much stronger.

## Protection

The final part of preparing your chamber requires that you protect the area, and yourself, from malevolent spirits and energies and anyone who might be psychically attacking you. It is imperative that you mentally and spiritually defend yourself, so taking these precautions will benefit you substantially.

Esoteric teachings prescribe to two primary methods of pro-

tection: first, performing all magickal workings within a consecrated circle; and second, performing a protection ritual from an
established grimoire. The circle, usually nine feet in diameter
(believed by Wiccans to represent the nine orders of the angels
and serve as a conduit for the power of Mars) is thought of as a
portable temple and is created for "drawing down the moon," or
again, extracting the power of the universe. Witches use incense
censers and create the protective circle beginning at the north.
They call on the gods to protect them while circling counter-
clockwise in the opposite direction, calling on all four points of
direction.

Magicians, on the other hand, form circles primarily for protection, and their ceremonies and rituals can be laborious and
very complex. Typically the circle is nine feet in diameter and has
a circle within the circle with a six-inch cutout to allow the magician to pass in and out. Biblical names of God, an altar, holy
water, and often a triangle that will hold evil spirits are also used.

As a corporate magician, you may prefer to use a simpler protective device that only requires you to draw a circle in the air
using your favorite business tool (I use my pen). Point the tool at
the bottom of your feet and recite the four corners of the wind as
you create the circle in the air. Do this one time. Then, do it
again, this time replacing the four directions with the following
words, while concentrating on building an impenetrable fortress
in which to do magick. Replace:

"North" with "Security"
"South" with "Success"
"East" with "Riches"
"West" with "Power"

Finally, ask the *Corporate Magick* Cabal to protect you from
all negative thoughts, malevolent spirits, psychic attacks, and personal enemies.

If you followed these simple steps, you have honed your magickal "sixth sense" to a degree where you'll be able to influence
the ethereal plane to do your bidding. You've also created your

magickal persona that is, in fact, your "inner magician"—the wizard you always knew was there but didn't know how to release. And you know how to prepare your sacred space and ritual chamber so that you can perform the amazing feats of corporate magick in a powerful corner office that resides not only here, but also in the magickal universe.

## CHAPTER 3

# The Corporate Hex-ecutive—
# Casting Spells the Wiccan Way

Witchcraft fits very well into the *Corporate Magick* model simply because most spells and workings in the craft are results-oriented. Considered "low magick" by some occultists because spells in Wicca are governed by natural laws and are usually not conducted with grand ceremony in order to affect the ethereal plane, they are nonetheless effective means to an end. And by virtue of spells' pragmatic workings, they hit the mark for corporate magicians who, after all, are most concerned with achieving business success. So, let's get right down to using your new-found wisdom by learning the basics of casting spells.

Keep in mind that a spell is the process of using your will along with selected tools to gain what you desire. Focus on your success, envision the outcome in your mind, believe wholeheartedly that it will happen, and launch the wish into the universe. When you couple your virulent imagination with tools like potions, herbs, and talismans, you'll set the stage for some powerful magick. It's a simple process, but one that requires the faith of the magician. Fortunately, you won't be relying totally on blind faith, because the testimonies of the people in this book reveal how they have used magick and made it work for them.

To bolster your confidence, consider that witchcraft is analogous to business from the standpoint that it uses a workplace (an altar), research (spells), tools (potions, herbs, oils, talismans), and deadlines (moon cycles and seasons) to achieve results. These "familiar" methods allow the corporate magician to customize his needs using the many ingredients, potions, spells, and charms from witchcraft with some modern-day modifications. For example, you may use a favorite pen as a talisman but charge it with traditional Wiccan blessings.

---

## CASE STUDY
## BELL, BOOK AND BUSINESSWOMAN

---

Jenny, a contemporary witch, used the techniques of the craft to help her in her publishing career. More a witch by modern definition than any particular Wiccan religious bent or sect, Jenny was editor in chief of a heavy-metal rock magazine—a job she'd wanted all her life. But her dream was in jeopardy. In the early days of her career, she merely dabbled and "played" with magick. She said, "I wasn't really a witch in those days. I was interested in magick but I didn't get very involved in what it was all about. I was really too busy with my magazine."

That soon changed. After about a year of being saddled with the myriad details of magazine publishing and feeling the slings and arrows of traditional corporate backstabbing, Jenny knew she needed help beyond what was traditionally available. She recalled how people in her company resented her quick rise; she'd experienced psychic attacks from all directions. "I intuitively felt that people were trying to sabotage the magazine and me personally. I knew for a fact that another woman practiced magick, and rumors were flying about how she used it against me. I tried all the regular paths—working harder and longer hours—and even tried some political moves, but the attacks became so intense, I knew I needed more 'unorthodox' help," she said.

On a short getaway trip to Salem, Massachusetts, a place where she always planned to visit to further study the occult, Jenny stopped at Crow Haven Corner, then the shop of well-known witch Laurie Cabot. Upon leaving the shop, Jenny locked eyes with Cabot as they were both walking up the block and immediately exchanged greetings. Something electric and mystical filled the air. In Jenny's mind, this was the defining moment that began her on her magickal path. She gathered books and ritual items from Salem and left with magick on her mind.

On her return to New York, Jenny studied all she could on Wicca, candle magick, spells, and potions with the intention of using spells and magick to aid her career. Although she never joined a coven, choosing instead to be an independent (solitary practitioner) witch, Jenny practiced the arts diligently. And her practice paid off.

During her second year as editor of the magazine, sales hit a financial high, but staff members continued to resent Jenny's success. That one backstabbing woman launched a serious attack on Jenny and the magazine in the hope of destroying what Jenny had built. "I found some personal belongings missing that had no monetary value, and strange powders were sprinkled around my desk and office," Jenny said.

With the aid of some magician friends, Jenny began protection and cleansing rituals. One such ritual she gleaned from a witch's grimoire consisted of her writing her nemesis' name on a piece of paper and putting it in a vial mixed with holy water, protection oil, and four thieves vinegar. She then folded the paper three times while pointing it away from her body and buried it on her private property under a full moon. For insurance, during the following waning moon, she dug up the paper and threw it into a body of running water that carried it downstream.

She also used candle magick to secure the financial well-being of the magazine during the stressful period. "I am a big supporter of the Anna Riva candle instruction books. My green candles were rubbed with prosperity oil, and the spell kept sales in the black. In addition, I used black and white candles dressed with appropriate oils for purification and to achieve my goals. I remember the scenario vividly by the two different candles working together," she recalled.

On a crisp, cold November night with the moon in full glow, Jenny went about conducting her prosperity spell. With her candles burning atop her stone altar, Jenny slowly rubbed the prosperity oil up and down the green candle from the center—the standard practice for achieving positive results. She alternately meditated while staring at the candle's flame and the cover of her magazine to assure that the power of the candle magick was moving though her and into her magazine. She recounted how she felt during the ceremony: "After about ten or fifteen minutes, I felt my mind become lost in the candle's flame. I saw it dance and flicker and was literally mesmerized by its beauty. Then, from nowhere, I saw in my mind that my foe was having great difficulty in the office—I could actually see and feel her becoming increasingly disturbed and disorganized, throwing things around, and cursing her own ineptitude. Then I saw the sales reports of my magazine for the year indicating that we had the most prosperous year ever. The two scenarios blended in my mind and at that instant I felt a surge of power—a little tingle—run though my spine. I knew the spell had taken effect."

It never entered Jenny's mind to wonder whether it was the actual rituals, or the fact that her nemesis knew Jenny was enlisting magick in her cause, that made her magickal recipes work. The results were positive. Her disgruntled employee was so involved and obsessed with Jenny's magickal defense that she neglected her duties at the company. When the publisher got wind of her ineptitude, he ordered her fired.

The magazine continued on its prosperous way, and Jenny solidified her career as a rock music journalist—and witch. To this day, she keeps an empty vial in her desk drawer—just in case.

---

# Let's *Spell* It Out

To reiterate, casting spells falls into the magickal category of "low" magick, that which provides a means to a tangible end as opposed to an attempt to attain higher spiritual fulfillment. Spells require the magician to use tools, timing, and verbal commands. The combinations of these aids—how one affects the other—are often referred to as their "aspects." The energy with which the spell is cast is the catalyst that sends the spell into the universe and ultimately changes the physical surroundings. As I've said, "supernatural" forces that make spells work are really the psychic energies of the magician. So, you need to gather your tools, focus, believe, and then work your spell.

Remember, using "unbusinesslike" tools and believing in your actions is not as foreign as you may think. I'm sure that in your everyday workaday dealings, you may wear that lucky tie to an important meeting, or keep a special charm in your pocket that has brought you luck in past negotiations. And don't forget your intuition. No doubt many of your best decisions were based on "gut feelings" alone, which are tantamount to your strong beliefs or faith. So you see, you're using your own spell-casting "tools" all the time. What you will be doing in the *Corporate Magick* system is adding new magickal tools and a time-tested structure to making things happen according to your will.

Age-old Wiccan spells and charms have been designed to work for everything from simple good fortune to raising the dead to call on their power. Of course, I'm sure there are some people in business whom you'd rather keep dead than raise, but my point in this chapter is that we'll apply the *effects,* the power of these spells, to your needs. But bear in mind that a basic tenet of witchcraft is that any spell thrown will return to the magician three times. If your goal is to wreak havoc or cause destruction, then, think again about casting it. It's probably not worth the trouble. Having said that, however, casting a spell for self-defense in most cases *is* justifiable.

A great deal of what *Corporate Magick* borrows from witchcraft is its reliance on sympathetic magick—that is, "like produces like." For example, we know the color of money in the United States is green, so although candle magick colors vary from one magickal discipline to another depending on the desired results, we will use green as our candle of prosperity. Again, it's the magician's energy that will direct the spell; the color is only an aid. And instead of using a ceremonial knife or athame to direct energies, you may use your favorite letter opener. You can blend accepted knowledge with any item that you feel will be a conduit for success because *you will charge it with your own energy.*

## Casting Spells—What You Need to Get the Job Done

Jenny, the magazine editor who used magick to save her magazine, showed how the power of witchcraft's magickal workings got results. Here's a breakdown of the tools and the times you'll need to conduct any spell aimed at magickal success. (*Note:* Wherever it's simpler to purchase already-made ingredients, like oils and powders, a reference is made to particular products.)

The basics for spell casting are listed below, followed by customized business spells for particular results. But if you can't wait and want to use the wily ways of Wicca immediately to advance your career, just consult the Instant Magick Index Card at the end of this chapter, which includes a basic magick "utility" that will work for any application. Or, for even faster application, use the *Corporate Magick* Quick Business Spell (also at the end of this chapter) prepared and tested effective in advance by the *Corporate Magick* Cabal.

## *Basic Spell-Casting Tools*

### Candles (large size)
Green (for money), blue (power), red (passion), black (defense).

### Energy Directors (Choose a favorite handheld instrument you use at work, such as a favorite pen, a paperweight, or a pointer.)

### Powders and Oils (Available at most occult shops, catalogs, or online stores. See Appendix: Resources.)
For success: success oil, willpower oil, millionaire oil/powder, patchouli oil, Wealthy Way oil/powder, green lodestone powder, King Solomon oil, command powder.
For protection: boss fix powder, devil's master, absinthe.

### Amulets and Talismans
Any small pouch, a lodestone, a lucky charm, a necklace, a poppet (or a small doll of any kind).

### Incense
Patchouli, success incense, Lucky John the Conqueror incense, prosperity incense, High John the Conqueror incense.

## Timing

### Moon Cycles

The moon has always held a high place in the magickal realm, primarily because it was the "ruler of the dark" and is at the core of witchcraft and many Pagan practices. And the gravitational pull of the moon directly affects life on earth, as is seen in the rising and ebbing of ocean tides. The two most important things you need to know about using the cycles of the moon in spell casting are its waxing and waning periods. A waxing moon is the "growing" period from dark moon to full moon; the waning moon is the "declining" period from full moon to dark moon. Spells designed to have a positive effect, such as a job promotion, should be conducted during the waxing moon. Spells conjured for closure, such as the end of a project, should be cast during the waning moon.

### Days and Hours

According to most grimoires, planets rule certain days of the week, and they each influence reality in their own way. For example, the planet Jupiter, a positive planet, rules Thursday and the hours of 1 and 8 of the day (A.M.), and 15 and 22 of the night (P.M.). It also influences riches and things desired. So spells for prosperity should be conjured during Jupiter's influence and its corresponding hours.

Because *Corporate Magick* is most concerned with your business success, I have homed in on the most powerful times for you to work your business magick and eliminated all of the "gray area" timeframes. I have personally tested spells during the following times and dates, and I'm convinced these periods are the best times for working your spells as well.

| Best Days | Best Hours | Influence |
|---|---|---|
| Thursday (Jupiter) | Day 1, 8; night 3, 22 | Riches, things desired |
| Sunday (sun) | (D)1, 3; (N)15, 22 | Fortune, hope |
| Wednesday (Mercury) | (D)1, 8; (N)15, 22 | Loss, debt (to reverse) |

# Six Common Areas for Business Spells

The *Corporate Magick* system has identified the six most common business scenarios that you'll probably face in the course of your career. Because these six essential areas are so results-oriented, they lend themselves perfectly to conducting spells. Remember, *Corporate Magick* spells are written, made, and used as a means to an end—a tangible end with measurable results. As I've already pointed out, spells can be carried out either through "high" (ceremonial) or "low" (natural) magick. Proponents of "high" magick, however, will argue that spells not carried out to the letter with all of the required pomp and recitations lose their meaning and will ultimately have no effect on either the ethereal or earthly plane. These same magicians also subscribe to the idea that the magician's will is the main ingredient for any working regardless of the spell, with which I agree. But they are adamant that the two must be combined or the spell is diminished. Are they right? Well, I believe ceremony was developed as "psychodrama" to get the magician in the right frame of mind so his will could be released into the universe. Let's just say the more you believe in what you're doing, regardless of the procedure, the more effective your working will be—whether it involves donning robes, banging gongs, and drawing circles of salt, or simply reciting an affirmation in your study.

## *The Six Business Scenarios*

1. **Projects.** In their simplest form, any project requires that you know what needs to be done, what resources and people are needed to facilitate the project, and what's required to get it done on time.

2. **Meetings.** Meetings are meant to form a plan of action or to discuss a particular problem or strategy. What you need to do here is show what you've got. It's like show-and-tell all over again.

3. **Personnel.** Managing people requires that you understand

different personalities and persuade them to think as the company thinks or motivate them to come up with new solutions.

4. **Budgets.** Budgets are self-explanatory. You have a limited amount of money to use to create a product, complete a project, or run a department.

5. **Strategy.** Strategies are nothing more than well-thought-out plans designed to accomplish a company goal.

6. **Career advancement.** This is self-explanatory. Your success is on the line every hour you spend at work. You need plans and action.

Prepare your basic business spells with these areas in mind and you'll have a solid foundation of magick when almost any situation arises. Most necessary ingredients can be found in your local occult shop or on the Internet.

## *Preparation*

A major part of any magician's complete working is the physical and mental preparation already discussed in chapter 2. And although we've customized traditional preparation for the modern corporate magician, the basics *must* be practiced before a spell is put into action. Whether an initiate (rookie), adept (novice and better), or magus (master), magicians and mystics have known for centuries that in order to get in touch with the deepest recesses of the subconscious and inner spirit, some fundamental "exercises" are required. The subconscious and conscious together are the keys to any magickal working. The subconscious releases the willpower so it can do the magician's bidding, and the more the magician can do to get in touch with the deep subconscious—the pathway to the hidden realms—the better and more powerful the magick will be. To recap the preparation, this is what you need to do:

1. **Apply your sixth sense training by meditating.** Get yourself in a relaxed state of mind—do whatever you normally do

to get "lost in your thoughts" or "lost in the moment." To some it's the soothing sounds of music. For others it's the peace of gardening, while still others like to run until they hit that high called the "zone." Everyone can achieve this sense of mental abandonment. It's a euphoric and calming sensation all at once.

One method is to recall a secret word that has great meaning to you. It could be a child's name or a favorite book. But this word *must* have deep significance to you so that it triggers calm and peacefulness. Or, create and recite a mantra that is repetitive and articulates your business goal. For example, if you want a promotion, a mantra might be:

*I am strong and confident
and deserve the job
I am ready and willing
to become a star*

Recite this over and over until it's the predominant thought in your mind. Believe in what you're saying. You created the idea; you must believe that it's true. Witches have practiced this for centuries. The repetition and belief imprints in your subconscious the idea that opens the gates to your magickal will.

You can also focus on the "secret word" that lets you block out the world around you so that you can concentrate completely.

2. Create your power and tap your "mentor" for guidance.

3. Enter you chamber and seek protection from the *Corporate Magick* Cabal.

At this point you should feel an overall sense of calm and an attachment to another part of yourself. This is your entrance into your deep subconscious and the place where all your magick will originate. You must now visualize as vividly as possible the set of circumstances you wish to alter in accordance with your will, whether it be a physical place, an individual, or a scenario. As we learned from the witches' pyramid, you need to exercise "virulent imagination" to the point where you feel yourself a part of the imagining. Do this by recognizing colors, smells, and tactile sensations one at a time. If you picture a restaurant, smell the smells, hear the noise, taste the food in your mouth. You must believe that this is no longer simply a thought in your head; it now *is* reality. And it is here where you will change reality to suit your means. This sets the stage on the astral plane—the other reality of your mind—and is the basis for all works that will follow.

---

## CASE STUDY
## THE FORETELLING FLORIST

Amy used her "virulent imagination" by using a scrying mirror—a favorite aid in witchcraft—and actually changed her professional reality through this brand of magick. Always fairly successful in business since she began her entrepreneurial floral career in her teens, Amy especially loved arranging baskets for holidays and special occasions. Early in the 1990s, however, the floral business evolved from mainly mom-and-pop operations to large telephone and online businesses. Amy knew that she would have to develop an edge to stay competitive, but having neither the clout nor the capital of the large companies, Amy had to call on her special esoteric abilities to help foretell the future.

As a teenager in her New England hometown, she often experimented with predictions using a scrying mirror—a handheld looking glass that acts as a magickal portal into the future.

In the basement of her home at her secret Wiccan altar, Amy consulted a dusty grimoire that instructed her to copy the magickal names *S. Solam S. Tattler S. Echogordner Gematur* on the new mirror, which would aid her in foreseeing what was to be. The book further told her to take the mirror and place it at a fork in a road during an uneven hour, and then, on the third day, at the same place and the same hour, she could retrieve it and use it to her advantage. A warning in the book noted that her reflection couldn't be the first one she saw in the mirror; an animal was preferred. Amy's black cat, Samantha, became the perfect choice, and at the prescribed time she had the feline gaze into the looking glass in keeping with the spell. The cloudy-looking glass suddenly took on a different reflective quality that resembled tinted or smoked glass, but with a deeper center that almost appeared as a hole in the glass.

Back at home in her secret room and altar, Amy concentrated on the mirror, gazing deeply into its void. In her mind's eye, she saw that the large conglomerate didn't offer custom-made arrangements and that there was a definite opportunity for her. Lost in the reflections for nearly an hour, sweating and flushed, Amy saw in the magickal mirror that a widowed neighbor would approach in the near future asking for a very special floral piece—something the big company florists couldn't produce.

Within a week of her vision, the bereaved person from Amy's clairvoyant episode approached her and asked for the special floral arrangement—a befitting farewell for her husband. A bit surprised but not shocked, Amy swiftly delivered a beautiful piece of work that she had been planning in her mind since her revelation. The old woman was pleasantly shocked and commented to Amy that it was as though she had read her mind. The word got around town about Amy's custom care and her uncanny "intuition" about what the old woman needed. Amy's business subsequently flourished under its new name, "Future Floral Arrangements."

---

## Basic Business Spells

Find a private area where you can set up your "altar." This area is preferably where you do business, either on your desk at home, a study, or ideally in your office at your workplace. You must prepare yourself with your own form of meditation beforehand for at least fifteen minutes. Spells can be repeated as many times as necessary. Remember, all spells can take days or even weeks to "kick in," so be patient.

These are Wiccan-based spells that will cover most business situations. After a while you will be able to substitute your own ingredients—those you feel have significance to the working desired. And once you have a "feel" for the timing, and the necessary intensity in your spell casting, you will be able to move on to more specific and advanced spells that you can create with some experimentation. As soon as you master a particular discipline's approach to working magick, you can begin to mix and match or work many spells from each school to achieve your desired goal. Don't worry about the orthodoxy of one school or another—the key is your desire.

## Spell for Completing a Project

**Ingredients:** Patchouli incense, red candle, success oil, energy director.

**Action:** Dress (rub with hand or cloth) the red candle with success oil from the middle upward (rubbing middle to top signifies positive movement and gain, while rubbing downward is to accomplish a negative result).

On any Thursday evening during the cycle of a waxing moon, light the candle at 8 P.M. and burn patchouli incense. Hold your energy director in your stronger hand, and for the first fifteen minutes, gaze directly into the candle flame, visualizing the successful completion of the project. See the results in your mind and see yourself closing a file or congratulating your coworkers on a job well done. After the first fifteen minutes, recite the following verse nine times (remember, you can create your own mantras also) without interruption.

> *Project large, project small*
> *It is in my power to finish all*
> *Results and praise will be the end*
> *Complete success I'll achieve again*

When through, *do not* blow out the candle, but fan it out with your hand.

## Spell for a Successful Meeting

**Ingredients:** Two blue candles, success oil, and success incense; something that will be used at the meeting (notes, pen); a talisman bag you will take with you.

**Action:** Dress the candles with success oil from the middle upward. Inscribe your wishes in the candle wax with a pointed instrument (preferably your energy director). Light the candle and incense for seven consecutive days before the meeting. Each evening, speak the results you desire from the meeting aloud, letting your breath lightly blow the candle flame while you're talking (be careful not to get too close). It would be best to light the candles at the same hour that the meeting is scheduled. Let the candles burn for an hour. On the eve of the meeting, place the ingredients for the meeting in your talisman bag and place it between the two candles. Allow the candles to extinguish themselves and bring the "charged" talisman bag with you to the meeting.

---

## CASE STUDY
## QUOTH THE RAVEN

---

Many salespeople live on intuition, and Scott was no exception. His gut feelings often helped him close a deal. But when insurance policy sales started to slip in his territory, the bachelor salesman became lonely and depressed. Scott's only chance to save his career was to shine in an important meeting with the director of sales for his company. He knew that if he impressed his boss, he could gain a more lucrative territory and a fat raise, not to mention keep his job. He had to make some key decisions about how to conduct the meeting and how he could blow his boss away, but he realized he needed some help.

Scott remembered that as a child he had often been comforted by his pet raven, Charlie. He recalled how Charlie would help him make decisions using what he'd called "magick" as a child. He would bring the bird into his darkened room, light some candles, concentrate deeply, and ask the bird questions. He said that an old woman, who lived down the street from him and was rumored to be a witch, told him that animals in some cultures were treated as magickal entities that were said to be the vessels of spirit gods. She whispered that ravens had particularly strong powers, and if he concentrated hard enough, the bird would point to objects that would help him. Although the woman was scorned by many in the area and passed off as crazy, Scott enjoyed her company and always felt she possessed a curiously strange inner knowledge.

So when Scott visited a local Fort Lauderdale pet shop looking for a new friend, a raven that had been for sale for almost two years rekindled his memory and caught his eye. He asked the owner why no one had bought the bird and was sharply told that it had been abandoned after an old neighborhood woman (coincidentally also known to dabble in witchcraft) had passed away and left the bird without a home.

Encouraged by the witch story and the possibilities that this bird was really a vessel of benevolent spirits, Scott bought the raven and named him Chucky in memory of his childhood friend. Remembering how his old pet had helped him in the past, Scott gave his old practices a try in an effort to win back some sales and a new plan or success.

He prepared his apartment walls with sheets of paper listing his recent prospects and began gathering objects for his makeshift altar. Scott bought large blue candles (for prosperity) and dressed them with success oil purchased at a local New Age shop. He quieted his chamber and began visualizing great sales and new opportunities that included a promotion and even relocation to a larger city. Upon lighting the candles, Chucky the raven mysteriously began fluttering around the room as if he knew Scott was contacting a higher power. Scott concentrated on the points he wanted to express and wrote them on profitable sales reports he had taken from the office. He then called up some old affirmations he remembered from his childhood attempts at magick and repeatedly recited them as he pasted the reports to the walls. He then focused on the bird, asking the raven to peck on the sales sheets that were most promising.

After about fifteen minutes of Scott's deep concentration, the fluttering black bird screeched and flew around the room, pecking on the same three sheets time after time. Scott knew that these sheets must contain some important information that he should use in his meeting—key companies he should contact.

The next day, Scott called on the "chosen" companies and was surprised, but not shocked, to discover that the bird had led him to information that would be crucial in his meeting with his manager. In all three cases, the contacts had been planning on moving their business to other firms—but Scott's concern convinced them otherwise. The salesman used this magickal information in his meeting with his supervisor, and it proved to be his saving grace.

The salesman's new magickal friend convinced him to once again begin practicing his special brand of magick, an avocation that vaulted him to director of sales for his company, relocation to a major city, and a new, larger home for his special friend Chucky.

## *Spell for Personnel Matters*

**Ingredients:**  Red candle (to help) and black (to reverse); Lucky John the Conqueror oil, poppet doll; a personal possession of the person you want to affect.

**Action:**  On a Sunday at 3 P.M. during the waning or waxing cycle of the moon (depending on your desired result—waxing for positive results, waning for reversal), dress the appropriate candle with John the Conqueror oil. Prepare the poppet doll with your intended person's personal item (ideally something organic—hair or fingernail clippings). Write on a piece of paper torn from that person's correspondence (letter, memo, note) what you wish to occur and attach it to the poppet. Place the poppet in front of the burning candle. If you desire help for that person, recite the following during a waxing-moon cycle:

> *Three times three\**
> *What is done to you*
> *Three times three*
> *Give help to you*
> *Three times three*
> *Bring the best to you*

If you wish to hinder a person's action, recite this verse during a waning-moon cycle:

> *Nine times nine\**
> *In very short time*
> *Nine times nine*
> *The reverse is mine*
> *Nine times nine*
> *My wish, your mind*

---

\*The numbers three and nine have significant magickal properties based on the Roman Catholic Holy Trinity and the multiplication of that power.

## Spell for Budgets or Gathering Money

**Ingredients:**  Green candle, millionaire oil, Wealthy Way powder, patchouli powder, green lodestone.

**Action:**  On a Thursday at 8 P.M. or 3 A.M. during a waxing-moon cycle, dress a green candle (a seven-knob candle with seven wicks is preferred) with millionaire oil and light for seven consecutive days. On the seventh day, mix together patchouli powder and Wealthy Way powder and sprinkle this on the lodestone. Bury the lodestone or hide it with a piece of gold or silver either in a talisman bag (red) or a silver or gold box. Dig it up only after the money has come or the budget has been approved.

## Spell for Strategy

**Ingredients:**  Command powder, a talisman necklace or charm, Lucky John the Conqueror incense.

**Action:**  Prepare with deep meditation for at least thirty minutes. Do not try to reach a strategy; think only of all of the elements involved. Burn the Lucky John incense, continue meditating, and let your mind wander freely for another thirty minutes. Take your necklace or charm and dust it with command powder. Wear or carry the talisman constantly for seven days. On the seventh day, repeat the first step, but now concentrate on the desired strategy.

## Spell for Career Advancement

**Ingredients:**  Success oil, willpower oil, blue candle, a favorite pen as an energy director, your resumé.

**Action:**  On any given Sunday at 1 P.M. or 3 A.M., light the candle dressed from the bottom up with willpower oil. Place the candle on top of your resumé so that it drips onto the paper. Dress your energy-director pen with success oil and write your strengths on a piece of paper. Inscribe your wishes into the candle wax with your energy director (if possible). For one week, light the candle every day and rewrite your strengths on the paper until you have written them seven times each.

---

## CASE STUDY
## THE DARK DARLING OF WALL STREET

---

She fancies herself a vampire nowadays, sleeping in a coffin and sometimes even using blood for certain magickal rituals. But despite being a "creature of the night," this modern magician uses the basics of witchcraft by day to do business with some of the financial world's heaviest hitters.

As a talented graphic artist in the mid 1980s, the "Black Rose"— as she is affectionately known—had gone from providing freelance computer graphics work within a prestigious Wall Street firm to running one of the first three computer graphics companies ever created in New York City. Though she never graduated from high school, Rose convinced the conservative company management to set her up in business and, within a few months, she had amassed a clientele that included some heavy-hitting companies. She did it with her talent and sixteen-hour workdays, but also with the help of magick, which she says she uses in every aspect of her life, *especially* in her business dealings.

"I managed to run a very successful computer graphics business in the mid-1980s, right in the middle of the crash," Rose told me. "I was earning a six-figure salary and I lived in a gorgeous apartment with two working fireplaces and a huge eighteen-foot skylight where I slept under the magickal stars. I even owned my own white stretch limousine and had a private driver."

How did she do it? A little candle magick for success and a lot of willpower. She began her plan with simple rituals designed to help her visualize the outcome of her corporate quests. Rose used colored candles of her own design based on past experiences, opting not to follow any prescribed candle magick book or advice from the corner occult shop. She knew what colors were supposed to work based on books and spells from her own library. But more importantly, she knew that the candles were often secondary to the amount of will she injected into the work. For example, she was aware that blue candles were commonly used for healing and prosperity purposes, but observed in her magickal dealings that white candles worked better in conditions of grave distress. So whenever Rose enlisted the power of candle magick, she experimented and, in effect, devised her very own candle magick discipline.

Her magickal quest for success began when Rose prepared her private altar with three candles: one for persuasion, one for finance, and one for strength, all "dressed" with specially prepared oils. She rubbed the candles with oil from the center outward to charge them with her intentions. "I felt that I had more energy from the center of my being, so it made sense to dress the candles from their center, too." She then carved her needs into the very core of the candles and focused her will on bending the very rigid plane of corporate reality.

Rose chose to harness the power of the full moon by conducting her spell in the moon's fullest cycle. She knew that her body responded best to the moon's gravitational pull at this time, so she personally felt full of power. She stared into the flame and visualized receiving all that she asked for. "I was careful to ask for only that which I needed to get the deal. Not because I was afraid of the bad karma or anything, but I know sometimes there are hidden results from using selfish magick."

Over a period of about five weeks, she conducted secret daily rituals also thanking her personal deity Atziluth, who is associated with the burning spirit of the Kabbalah.

By evening of each day she visualized the company executives meeting with her and giving her the space she needed to begin her business. "The flame talked to me. The way it moved told me when I should press an issue or hold back. A steady yellow hue meant stay the course while I summoned my wishes, while a red flare told me I should take strong action." The barometric effect of the flames are common indicators in candle magick and ultimately proved to be on the money for Rose as well.

She then projected into her partners' minds the thought of herself sitting in an office on Wall Street and conducting her new business from a comfortable executive chair, along with thoughts of how her business would help them succeed. Within a few days after her last working, the management at the Wall Street firm offered Rose space to work. But it didn't stop there. Management actually built a *new* office for her rent-free, giving Rose and her fledgling company a prestigious place of its own. And what's even more astounding is that her new space was created despite the fact that the company already had its own in-house graphic art department on the same floor. If that's not magick, what is?

# Get to Work!

The spells and case studies in witchcraft here should give you a good overview of how to apply witchcraft to your own brand of *Corporate Magick*. They cover most business situations, but after a while, as you've seen from other case studies, you will be able to substitute your own ingredients—those you feel have significance to the magickal working desired. Once you have a "feel" for the timing and the necessary intensity in your spell casting, you will be able to move onto more specific and advanced spells that can be created by you with some experimentation. There are hundreds of books on witchcraft and many, many exacting spells from the world's oldest religion. I encourage you to experiment and talk to others in the craft. You will find that witches are very pragmatic and work many spells for the good of themselves, their friends, and for prosperity. My advice is to think about what you want from your career this very moment and perform some magick. You'll be pleasantly surprised to find that within a short period of time, you will become comfortable about being a corporate magician and you'll be amazed how effective your spells really are.

## INSTANT MAGICK INDEX CARD

### How to Cast a Spell

**Ingredients:** Candles: green (riches), black (defense), red (passion), white (negotiation); frankincense incense.

**Ceremony:** Find a secluded space and place a candle the color of your desire in the center of the table. Light frankincense incense.

**Action:** Meditate and clear your mind of daily distractions. During a waxing (growing) moon, be sure you're facing east and light the candle. Concentrate on its flame for at least fifteen minutes, seeing your desired result becoming true.

### *Corporate Magick* Quick Business Spell

Take an index card and draw a solid green circle. As you are drawing it, call on the *Corporate Magick* Cabal asking for power (the Cabal is psychically attuned to its name). In a secluded space, stare at the circle for fifteen minutes while visualizing your desired results.

# CHAPTER 4

# Talismans, Charms, and Amulets

We all have them—lucky charms, favorite articles of clothing, special coins, religious medals, inanimate objects with which we associate special powers that will bring us good fortune or protect us from evil. Everyone has had a rabbit's foot or St. Christopher medal close at hand at one time or another. We usually believe these charms and talismans are supernaturally charged, and if carried during a time of need will help bring us luck or help us though some trying experience.

Of all of the occult practices in our culture, "lucky charms" are the most benign magickal items, accepted even by those who discount any part of the magickal world as simple superstition. And there's good reason for this acceptance: A talisman or amulet is usually given to someone from a person he cares a great deal about, or is associated with a special emotional situation. The emotional attachment sets up a psychic connection that affects the ethereal plane and helps out the bearer of the charm. In other words, carrying or giving amulets and talismans is simply another form of performing magick.

And what supercharges this type of magick is powerful belief—more often considered faith in the world of charms, it is still primarily the stuff of magick. For centuries, people have been transferring their beliefs to their favorite charms. This powerful association is, in fact, a method of "blessing" an object so it retains the magick for use at a later time. Prehistoric peoples would use the bones and skins of animals that they perceived as gods in order to gain the animal's power through transference, and thus believed that they became godlike themselves. Carved wooden and stone images also had a place in early man's fascination with objects thought to be magickal. It was reasoned that if a miniature likeness resembled something powerful, then it must contain that power, albeit on a smaller scale. Our early fascination with statues, charms, amulets, and talismans became deeply rooted in our psyches and included everything from four-leaf clovers and rabbit's feet to religious items such as the Christian crucifix. And so it is with business as well. We have our lucky ties and blouses and all of us, at one time or another, have used our special pen given by a loved one at graduation. We give these items power with our own beliefs, and the magick becomes real.

There should be a distinction made here as to the literal meaning of all of the magickal charms, because they are often used interchangeably. In occult jargon, a charm is usually a spoken incantation that's voiced to act as the catalyst for a spell. However, the term "charm" is commonly known as a small trinket worn around the neck or on a bracelet. Or a charm can be a voodoo *gris-gris* bag, which is a small pouch containing an odd number of materials (no more than thirteen). A charm can also be the spoken blessing performed over an object such as a talisman or a fetish.

A charm used as a blessing rite can range from something as simple as wishing your results while imagining a desired outcome, to more elaborate ceremonies based on ancient magickal prescriptions that can contain ingredients such as herbs, incense, water, and special parchments. The time of day, the cycles of the seasons, and the moon are also ceremonial aspects of charms—depending on what is to be accomplished.

You should also be aware that the terms "talisman" and "amulet" are often used interchangeably, but they do have specific qualities. An amulet is used, in most cases, for protection;

talismans as catalysts for some desired result. So, a magickal object can be both an amulet and a talisman, and in some cases, even a fetish. Sounds a bit confusing, but what you'll discover is that in the world of the corporate magician, how the object is charged is more important that what it's called.

---

## CASE STUDY
## A CHARMING ATTORNEY

---

Some lawyers would lead you to believe that to win a lawsuit, an attorney must do intense research, find flaws in his opponent's arguments, present a convincing case, and have a bit of luck thrown in. But Allen, an Atlanta attorney for more than ten years, studied more arcane kinds of books than those available in the local law library and knew he could count on the other, more mysterious powers contained in those ancient tomes to do his bidding.

Allen was hired to prove that his client was innocent of charges that he'd been driving while intoxicated and left the scene of an accident in which an elderly man had been struck and seriously injured. The case became difficult because the injured man was well liked in the community and had considerable influence among the local politicians. And although Allen gathered a good amount of evidence in favor of his client and knew he could deliver a tight case, he reasoned that he needed more than evidence to overcome a jury that might be sympathetic to the elderly victim.

The young attorney had secretly dabbled in the mystical sciences in the past and, on more than one occasion, enlisted magick to aid in his legal battles. Allen realized that because of the "bad-guy" image confronting him by defending an allegedly irresponsible driver, this particular case called for him to use two of his favorite spells: one to remove his enemies' strength by creating a special charm, and the other to assure victory in the courtroom.

A fan of voodoo, Allen's first step was to make his own special *gris-gris* bag charm that he could carry with him whenever he had a meeting with other lawyers or when he entered the courtroom. The ingredients in the *gris-gris* bag had to have some significance to the case, so Allen made it his business to secure a piece of the original signed testimony from the defendant. He knew that the defendant personally handled the papers, so microscopic pieces of his skin were still on the document. Hair, nails, and skin are powerful magickal conduits and essential ingredients in the type of magickal *gris-gris* Allen was using.

In addition to the piece of paper, the special bag—made out of chamois—also contained special ingredients of success that Allen worked with in the past, including success oil and herbal ingredients traditionally used to attract riches such as St. John the Conqueror root, one teaspoon of buckeye, a teaspoon of silverweed, a tablespoon of five finger grass, and one of Allen's Bar Association lapel pins. Armed with his special aid, Allen was now prepared to make his case.

A *gris-gris* bag must be anointed with the proper oils during the charging ritual, so the night before his court appearance, Allen closed his study door and anointed the bag with success oil. He proceeded to light white and black candles—white for purity and black for deliverance—and recited a spell aimed directly at draining the strength from his rival. As the candle flames danced in front of his eyes, Allen recited the following enchantment three times: *"I Allen, breathe on thee, three drops of blood I draw from thee. The first from thy heart, the other from thy liver, the third from thy vigorous life."* He concluded his ritual by bellowing *"By this I take all thy strength both mind and sinew!"*

The next morning, Allen applied the second charm. This had religious significance he'd once thought odd, but now made sense because of successful past workings. As prescribed by his secret books, he wrote the names of the twelve Christian apostles on large sage leaves, placed them in his shoes, and walked confidently into the courthouse.

Although he felt a great deal of hostility from the jury and at times from the judge himself, Allen's confidence in his knowledge—backed up with his *gris-gris* bag and magickally prepared shoes—gave him the necessary edge to present a convincing case for his client.

Within two hours of the closing arguments, the jury announced that it found the defendant innocent. The swift acquittal caused Allen to curl his toes in his shoes, kneading the leaves as the judge freed his client.

## Instant Magick Index Card

### How to Make a Charm

**Ingredients:** A cloth bag; items significant to the desired result (such as a coin if money is desired). Include an odd number of items in bag, no more than thirteen; white and green candles; success oil.
**Ceremony:** Light a white and green candle, anoint the bag with success oil, and place it between the candles.
**Blessing:** Fill the bag with the ingredients while imagining a successful outcome. Leave the bag between the candles for at least an hour, and then extinguish the flames.
**Action:** Carry the bag or place it in the area in need of the magick.

### *Corporate Magick* Quick Business Charm

Place your business card (or any personal card) in this closed book on a Thursday evening. Ask the *Corporate Magick* Cabal to psychically empower your charm.

# Talismans

The most ambiguous of the portable magickal tools is the talisman. Although they are often physical objects, they can also be simple incantations alone, or a combination of verse and object. The key to talismans is that they are the catalysts for magickal power. Where charms and fetishes actually "hold" the magick power, talismans are the "on/off" switches that usually require the magician to act with words or some manipulation of their ingredients before they will work.

## CASE STUDY
## THE TALI-"SALES"-MAN

Using a talisman found in an old magickal grimoire from his local library, Morris managed to land a new job in a local Detroit car dealership, despite his colleagues constantly telling him he'd never make the grade.

Although he had many years of experience as a car salesman, Morris had never made the jump from floor salesman to manager. He was a successful salesman, but during his tenure at three different dealerships, upper management never recognized his full potential. In Morris's mind he knew he had what it took to get the promotion and pay raise, but something always seemed to hold him back. After hearing from a "very mystically minded" friend that the very act of creating a blessing and bestowing that blessing onto an object that can be carried on your person can have profound effects on your life, Morris decided to do a little research into the mystical arts and see for himself. He figured he had nothing to lose, and if his friend was right he'd be "blessed" in more ways than one.

Morris's magickal quest took him to the local library, where he found an interesting old Saxon magick book from the Middle Ages, which instructed a person on how to become a leader in battle by creating a specific talisman. Morris thought that by creating and modifying the talisman to his needs, he could become a leader in his profession.

The rather odd-looking book, tattered and moldy, instructed Morris to gather some uncommon ingredients for the first part of the talisman, including a block of myrrh incense and a piece of flint. Not everyday items for sure, but with some diligent shopping he managed to secure them nonetheless. The remaining ingredients—a hawk feather and some bull hide—proved to be a bigger challenge. Morris did secure a hawk feather being sold on a Native American Web site, and improvised the bull hide by using a piece of discarded leather from an automobile being repaired in his dealership's service shop. He reasoned that the leather was close enough to the bull hide and actually had more significance to his auto industry goals. He also knew that he could carry the leather wherever he went, and it would always be charged with his magickal energy and will.

With the ingredients secured, Morris followed the book's instructions, which required the talisman to be held over the burning myrrh incense on the first Tuesday of the month at the stroke of midnight (the planetary day of Mars, named by the Romans more than two thousand years ago for their god of war). Morris recited the simple phrase, *"I have the knowledge, the personality, and the strength to become a manager,"* numerous times while holding the leather over the smoking incense for one full hour, as instructed in the book.

Morris carried the leather talisman in his suit jacket for the next few weeks and, on the first Tuesday of the following month, allowed the magick to do its work. On the spur of the moment that Tuesday afternoon, Morris asked his boss to consider him for a manager's position when the next opening occurred.

Today, Morris is a key executive at one of Detroit's most prestigious car dealerships. He *was* given the manager's spot at his job, but within two months he was wooed away by a rival company for more money and a better title—director of sales. Morris used magick and the corporate doors opened wide.

---

## INSTANT MAGICK INDEX CARD

### How to Make and Use Talismans

**Ingredients:** An object that can be associated with the desired result—for example, a pen if you need to write an important report.

**Blessing:** A spoken or thought phrase, poem, or rhyming incantation that expresses the desired results.

**Ceremony:** An area of solitude where the blessing can take place. Preferably in the office or area where the talisman is to do its work.

**Action:** During a waxing (growing) moon, say the blessing over the talisman at least three times while envisioning the desired result. Place the charged object in a pocket close to your body at least an hour before the event. Or, place the talisman in the physical area. During the event the talisman will do its magickal work.

### *Corporate Magick* Quick Magick Business Talisman

Get the front page of any Thursday *Wall Street Journal*, fold it three times, place it behind a picture of a loved one, and summon the *Corporate Magick* Cabal to do the work.

## Fetishes

Another magickal accessory, although less common, is a "fetish." Originating from the Latin word *faticius*, it refers to anything artificially made by the sorcerer's hand. The word also has roots in the Portuguese word *feitico*, which actually translates to "magick." So despite its most common definition connoting a sexual obsession (which it can be), a fetish, for *Corporate Magick* purposes, is a man-made magickal instrument.

Magickal fetishes have their origin in primitive Africa, where they were a common witch doctor's tool believed to contain the actual spirits of the gods, both good and evil.

A fetish blessing includes a number of basic elements, including:

- The fetish itself (a wooden statue, animal part, stones, bags made of animal skins).
- A spoken incantation, blessing, or charm.
- Candles, incense, or other "mood" enhancers.
- A magickal practitioner (in our case the corporate magician).

The choice of the fetish should have significance to the desired outcome. For example, if you intend for the fetish to protect you in a meeting with accountants, you might want your fetish to be a small calculator or some other financial object. Remember, you will charge the item with your belief, and that will make it powerful.

---

## CASE STUDY
## A FETISH FOR NUMBERS

---

Sarah, an accountant for a major New York firm, used a favorite fetish of hers when she found herself in a precarious situation that threatened her partnership standing. Her personal magickal aid— a mummified chicken's foot—is an odd item even for those accustomed to the occult, but because Sarah could trace its roots back to her ancestors in Kenya, she was confident that it could help her in the most dire business situation. The chicken's foot has been handed down in her family for hundreds of years. Legend has it that an elder in Sarah's family tribe was once accused of stealing some valuable farming tools from one of the other tribe members. In retribution, the accuser summoned the tribe's witch doctor and had him curse Sarah's relative with seven years of poor farming in an effort to starve his family.

Sarah's relative countered the curse by taking the matter into his own hands, using a ceremony that asked the tribe's gods for protection by blessing a sacred article (a fetish). A chicken's foot was chosen as the fetish to be blessed because it represented farming and food—the very things his opponent was seeking to destroy. The fetish was used countless times, and the legend tells that it protected the man's family for the rest of their lives.

Having grown up on this story and been exposed to her native magickal traditions since she was a child, Sarah often takes advantage of the use of the mummified chicken foot. And although the original blessing ceremony of the fetish has been lost and changed over the years, the basic elements have been handed down to each generation. Sarah uses the basics of the blessing, and each time she's in need of the fetish's power she modifies the incantations to suit the circumstances.

This time Sarah needed to protect herself from a company rival bent on making her look incompetent, trying everything in her power to prove Sarah's accounting practices wrong, or to question her judgment concerning a client's tax strategies. In most cases Sarah held her own and never really appeared to be in danger, but when her nemesis deliberately told one of Sarah's clients that Sarah was taking drugs, the gloves were off. It was time for Sarah to resort to her magickal roots and put her fetish into action.

She gathered as many of her family photos and journals as she could muster and placed them in a circle on a prized wooden table she bought at an African gallery. Lighting her candles and reciting the tribal incantation that she recalled from her grandmother's tales, Sarah held the mummified chicken's foot and asked for its protection against the woman determined to destroy her career. She felt the fetish's power surge through her, all the while envisioning her ancestors dancing and blessing Sarah's magickal workings.

The next morning, with the fetish in her briefcase, Sarah sat at her desk confident that she was now protected against whatever her foe had up her sleeve. As the day went on, Sarah's boss told her that the client in question was coming by for a meeting in the afternoon and that Sarah should be prepared for a conference. Her boss said that the client was troubled about something and needed to speak with Sarah as soon as possible. Although the warning was unnerving, Sarah knew that her fetish—forged hundreds of years before with a power that protected her family from starving—was ready for action.

As it turned out, another firm member had come to Sarah's aid—unbeknownst to Sarah—and told the client that there had been harmful and untrue rumors spread about Sarah and that he should not believe a word. What's more, when Sarah's client heard that this other person was spreading lies, he asked the woman flat out if there was anything she knew about Sarah. Because he was prepared beforehand, he anticipated her lie and called her bluff, exposing her plot to ruin Sarah's reputation. The troublemaker broke down and offered her resignation. Sarah could almost hear the distant drums beating, certain that her magickal fetish protected her again.

## INSTANT MAGICK INDEX CARD

### Charging a Fetish

**Ingredients:** An object, preferably of natural origin such as a rock, feather, root, or animal part, such as bones or mummified parts.

**Blessing:** Fetishes are charged with spirits who do the magician's bidding. Identify the spirit (a departed loved one, god, known shaman, witch, or magician) and ask for his blessing and to transfer his power into the fetish.

**Ceremony:** Preferably performed with one candle in the dark. Concentrate on the candle while asking the spirit to charge the fetish. Keep a strong image of the spirit in mind at all times.

**Action:** Keep the fetish in your hand immediately before the event and fondle it repeatedly.

### *Corporate Magick* Quick Business Fetish

Purchase an eagle feather and dip it into a running stream at midnight. Offer it to the *Corporate Magick* Cabal.

# Amulets

Most people simply come upon a magickal amulet by chance or are given one as a gift. They are the best known of the "portable" magickal items because they have taken many forms over the centuries. By definition, an amulet is something worn, usually for protection. A talisman can also be worn but is more likely to be an object of some kind that can either be carried or placed on an altar or in a stationary place.

Amulets with innate powers are the stuff of legends. We know of the deadly Hand of Glory (a severed and preserved hand of a corpse) used in necromantic rites to raise the dead, as well as more benign and positive good-luck amulets like four-leaf clovers.

But the most powerful devices are the ones created by magicians themselves because they contain the ingredients specifically designed to achieve whatever goal is sought. No one knows better, or is capable of infusing an amulet with more specific power, than the magician performing his own magick.

---

## CASE STUDY
## AMU-LET IT HELP HER

---

Bill, an artist with a major commercial design company in Chicago, used his magickal skills to help a peer who was faced with major distress over a new and challenging project.

His friend and coworker Tiffany was a talented artist who possessed more than enough skill to accomplish the task of designing a new corporate image for a huge supermarket chain. But the stress of performing well and the ultimate responsibility of winning the account proved to be too much for her. She lost sleep, would eat very little, and was often stricken with stomach problems and headache whenever discussing the job.

Bill, however, was an old hand at using magick in just such circumstances, having used his own brand of *Corporate Magick* to further his career in trying times. He was always able to get the job done as a practicing solitary witch for nearly twenty years. So when he saw his good friend falling apart, he delved into his "bag of tricks" and remembered a particularly effective method of calming the business jitters. He decided to put his magickal skills to the test for a friend.

Bill recalled how pebbles washed smooth from a stream or the sea, called "patience stones," often helped him in times of need. He knew they had the potential of also helping Tiffany.

To become an effective amulet, the patience stones had to be placed in a bag and given as a gift to the person in need by a friend. So Bill began gathering the special pebbles from a local stream and created his own blessing in his mind while he collected them, all the while concentrating on the most serene and peaceful powers of nature that he could imagine.

During a waxing (increasing) moon, Bill washed a handful of his newfound pebbles, dried them carefully, and, while rolling them between his fingers and cupping them in his hands, meditated on Tiffany's image and recited the following blessing: *"Power of peace enter these stones. Smoothness of the pebbles smooth the path; permanence of rock bestow your patience."*

Bill concentrated on transferring the calming power of the stones from his mind into Tiffany's. He visualized her holding the stones while she presented the most creative and visually stimulating project of her career. Bill's mental image showed Tiffany laughing and being congratulated, all the while clicking the patience stones in her hands.

The intense ceremony left Bill drained, but he knew the power was now placed in the stones. The next step was to present them to Tiffany before a full moon. Although she thought it was odd that the two of them were standing outside in the cold of January under a full moon while Bill handed her a bag of pebbles, she knew the gesture was special, so she welcomed Bill's gift. And after a few moments she actually felt a surge of goodness and peace rise within her; the fear of the pending project diminished almost immediately.

When she asked him why he gave her such an odd gift, Bill explained that it was a specially charged and magickal amulet that would give her the necessary patience to complete her project successfully. She told Bill that it was funny, because just a few days before, she'd felt as though things were starting to calm down about work. Now, she said, she was sure. Bill didn't let on that those few days ago was the moment when he began blessing the stones to serve their new master in her difficult times. He knew that the magick had begun. It wasn't long before Tiffany created a presentation that wowed the supermarket chain's executives with the new corporate identity. And it just so happened that the new campaign included the word "magic" in its title.

---

## Instant Magick Index Card

### How to Make and Use Amulets

**Ingredients:** Amulets, used for protection, require that the ingredients have some proven magickal power. For example, mandrake root has known magickal qualities, especially for influence. Pieces of the root are used in sachets to ensure prosperity. So, you must first identify the correct ingredient for your desired result. Ask at your local occult shop. **Blessing:** Like any magickal object, it must be purified and charged with your power. Because amulets already have some innate powers, asking the universe to cleanse the object can purify them. Use incense during purification.

**Action:** Leave the amulet in a darkened area for at least three days, and then place it where you want it to work (possibly on your person).

## *Corporate Magick* Quick Business Amulet

Fill your briefcase or portfolio with St. John the Conqueror root along with this book during the full moon. The *Corporate Magick* Cabal will charge it with magick.

# CHAPTER 5

# Astrology—Success by the Stars

Come on, admit it. You read your horoscope in your daily newspaper to see how your day is going to shape up. Is your boss going to lay into you for something you left out of a report? Is it the right time to ask for a raise? You check out the horoscope just to be sure—whether you really believe it or not.

In fact, you've probably known your birth sign since you were a kid. Maybe on a wild whim, you even considered having your zodiac symbol tattooed on your body. Well, even if that isn't true, you have at some time in your life been mystified (or downright confused) by the workings of astrology and what it means for you.

The stars instinctively fascinate most people. It's estimated that one in every ten thousand people is involved in astrology as a student or a practitioner. Marcus Goodwin quotes in his book *The Psychic Investor* that more than forty million people in the United States read their daily horoscope. What's more, the hunger for astrology is not limited to the secretary on the bus or even the middle manager at your company. Large corporations have consulted the stars. There's a capitalist "urban legend," which says that Coca-Cola couldn't open its first bottling plant in Thailand until the brass consulted with astrologers who gave a green light. And a few years back, a major detergent company was accused of having occult symbols in its logo and using astrology in its business practices. Although the allegations were denied, rumor had it that the board of directors often used the stars to forecast earnings, predict successful product lines, and magickally spy on the competition. It has been said that financier J. P. Morgan often consulted Evangeline Adams, a noted late-nineteenth-century astrologer who won acclaim for predicting the devastating Hotel Windsor fire in New York. He apparently once quipped, "Millionaires don't use astrologers . . . but billionaires do." So if you think "Taurus" is just a lot of bull . . . think again.

If you had to boil down the whole world of astrology and horoscope readings into why it's so popular, you'd have to say that people want to know what the future holds in store for them. Give 'em a glimpse—good or bad—of what they can expect, and they feel they have at least some power over their usually mundane and haphazard lives.

Although astrology is not "operative" magick—its use will not directly alter reality by the will of the magician—it is akin to magick because it is a method of using the unseen universal powers to predict future events *and* influence individuals. And the *Corporate Magick* system adds to the method of using astrology for divination—or predicting the future by tapping into astrology's cosmic influences—by adding the element of low, "get-results," sympathetic magick. As my job is helping you advance your business career and success, I've modified astrology to work for you.

Because each zodiac sign has certain aspects, or qualities, we take advantage of those influences when conjuring sympathetic magick and the casting of spells. Knowing a person's astrological makeup will help determine how to conduct a successful working. For example, if a person's zodiac sign is Cancer, the magickal color for that sign is silver, so a silver object might be used in casting a spell.

Astrology is a discipline that can be downright daunting, with complicated mathematical computations necessary just to figure out under which sign you were born. Fortunately, *Corporate Magick* eliminates most of the drudgery, giving you the basic tools necessary to use astrology in business matters without all of the foreboding computations. Although it won't be necessary to know all of the terms and descriptions, the two branches of astrology that we will deal with are natal astrology, which directly affects a person, and mundane astrology, which deals with nations and large groups of people. You will be concerned with both types because you'll be working magick on individuals as well as businesses.

You will also need to know certain basic information, like your own astrological sign and its correspondences (gem or color), and how the planets and their "aspects" (similar to a person's character traits) affect your sign. But you won't have to do complicated charting. On the flip side, you'll also need to know how a company or other business associate's astrological position interacts with your sun signs.

So, to give you some perspective, let's recap some astrology basics from earlier chapters. The study of the stars began somewhere during Babylonian times, around 3000 B.C., or perhaps even before that. The Greeks, ancient Indians, the Mayans, and the Chinese (the Chinese zodiac is distinctly different from Western astrology, however) all used forms of astrology to predict the future and to discover signs of imminent disaster or prosperity. Early scientists, actually considered by some to be magicians, often consulted the movements of the stars and used the symbols of the zodiac in rituals. And of course the moon, a centerpiece of Pagan worship, has always had deep magickal significance that holds true to this day in the Wiccan community.

In its truest, albeit simplest sense, astrology, the forebearer of astronomy, gets its magickal due because it was the measuring tool for the cycles of life on earth. The sun and moon rise and set and influence the seasons. A full moon changes the ocean tides. The stars shine like gems, changing direction in the skies and resembling earthly figures, so ancient civilizations gave the heavens magickal credence. The pure belief in magick gives it its power, and belief and strong will together influence reality.

Astrology centers on the horoscope, a circular "pie" or map divided into thirty-degree sections, each with specific, commonly known sun signs. These twelve signs, called the signs of the zodiac, are symbols created from star constellations and are familiar to most people from their daily newspaper horoscopes. Each sign has a corresponding stationary "house" numbered one through twelve. The sun's rotation around the heavens is the catalyst that determines your sign. So if the sun passed through the house of Aquarius at your time of birth, you're considered an Aquarian. (There are other considerations as to the hour of birth that also influence astrological readings, but we will be only concerned with major attributes in order to work magick.)

In addition to its corresponding house, each sign has a number of other influences, including "aspects," ruling planets, elements (earth, air, fire, and water), and whether it's a masculine (aggressive) or feminine (passive) sign. All of these variables will ultimately affect an astrological working. So you can see, charting traditional horoscopes can be difficult enough for one individual's birth sign—never mind an entire company's standing. Although you'll have to take into effect all of these considerations when using *Corporate Magick*'s astrological approach, I've broken the system down into a manageable and more useful formula.

First, check the charts on pages 81 and 82 and note each sign and how its planet, house, and element affect it. Then, once you know your sign, or that of the person or company that's to receive your magick, you can predict the probable outcome of a future event or use their strengths or weaknesses to do your magickal bidding.

---

## CASE STUDY
## CALCULATING THE STARS

---

Michael, a management consultant for one of the Big Eight accounting firms, found that once he knew how to position himself in his company by using "star power," his success was assured. Although Michael was doing well at his job, he became very concerned about a high-level financial proposal he had to submit to a major client's board of directors. Because his company was cutting its workforce, a number of managers were faced with the frightening reality of losing their jobs if they weren't considered invaluable. So although Michael knew he would work many hours on his report and was confident that the findings were favorable for his client, he wanted to be sure that his analysis would keep him in good standing with his company's brass. His experience told him that often a good analysis had as much to do with a company's culture as with numbers alone. If the report "fits" with the company's philosophy, then the client knows the analyst did his homework.

So Michael's task was clear: He had to use his knowledge of the stars to help make his analysis a success.

Michael's interest in astrology stemmed from an early childhood experience when his mother, an avid horoscope enthusiast, had her natal (birth) chart prepared and discovered that Michael, her firstborn, was soon to be the recipient of great fortune. The eleven-year-old boy didn't think much of it, but when cleaning his grandmother's attic, he discovered a shoebox full of rare baseball cards—some worth as much as five thousand dollars. It forever changed his thinking. And since that experience Michael consulted the stars for every major life decision, from his marriage to his career.

Michael did some detective work to discover the zodiac sign of the person he had to impress with his report. He called his client's personal secretary and asked for his birthday under the ruse that he wanted to keep it in his client's "special days" file. Once he discovered that the executive was born under the sign of Taurus, he knew how to approach the situation. Taurus personalities are generally earthy (their element) and are governed by the second house of the zodiac that relates to stability, morals, money, possessions, and how they're used. Not a surprise for a financial captain of industry. But Michael also knew that Taurus's ruling planet is Venus, which posed an interesting dichotomy because the ruling planet Venus represents love, art, romance, and sentimentality.

So just with this amount of basic information, Michael was able to consult astrological guides and determine the executive's position in the heavens. Because he also used his own brand of sympathetic magick, Michael combined the two disciplines so that he could prepare a report that appealed to both the executive's conservative *and* his artistic side. He decided to dig a little deeper and consulted with an astrologer friend named Mandy, who cautioned him that in order to be accurate, many areas of the natal horoscope must be considered before determining what would impress his client. Although he knew his client's sign was a pure Taurus—his birth date fell on May 2—Mandy warned Michael that some astrologers chart by the dates of constellations, which differ slightly from the sun sign date. So although Taurus falls between April 21 and May 21, the "constellation dates" end on May 10. And to further complicate issues, there are borderline or "cusp" birth dates that could have an effect on an accurate conclusion.

But because Michael was a magician first, and subscribed to the *Corporate Magick* philosophy of using *all* esoteric disciplines as a means to an end, he instinctively knew that if he had the right general positioning of the stars, even if they weren't devised by precision astrological means, then universal magick would kick in and deliver the answers he needed.

Michael used the magickal principle I've already discussed called sympathetic magick, in conjunction with his astrological knowledge. "I reasoned that this guy was a true Taurus; he had all of the regular traits. He was conservative, steadfast, and valued the buck," Michael explained. "So I used astrology as sort of an 'energy booster' to help my magick work. I did a candle-burning spell and used the colors of his sign—earthy olives and oranges—as backdrops on the wall of my office chamber. The combination was positively explosive!"

He prepared his report with the Taurus executive's outstanding traits in mind. A combination of solid business analysis that contained substantial market research, coupled with an appreciation of art, would do the trick. He submitted his proposal to his client, advising him that the art world was ripe for professional accounting services, adding that his research had found many major art houses were concentrating far more on the creative end than the financial aspects of their business. He confidently recommended in his report that the Big Eight firm should pursue those types of companies.

And for added measure, because he knew from his astrological charts that the Taurus boss's lucky colors were pastel shades of blue, he used a pastel blue cover on the report. Within two weeks, the Big Eight firm notified the company that the report was excellent, and that they were pursuing companies in the art world. The letter also had a note attached to Michael's boss praising Michael for an outstanding job "full of extraordinarily valuable insight," which secured his position for a long time to come.

# Astrological Signs

Following you'll find each sign, the date when the sun entered its house, and its business-related "qualities":

| Sun Sign | Dates | Business Quality |
| --- | --- | --- |
| Aries | March 21–April 20 | Bravery and work ethic |
| Taurus | April 21–May 20, 21 | Patience and tenacity |
| Gemini | May 21, 22–June 21 | Strategy and ideas |
| Cancer | June 22–July 22 | Sensitivity and inspiration |
| Leo | July 23–Aug. 22, 23 | Power and intelligence |
| Virgo | Aug. 23, 24–Sept. 22, 23 | Logic and being methodical |
| Libra | Sept. 23, 24–Oct. 22, 23 | Management and details |
| Scorpio | Oct. 23, 24–Nov. 22 | Ruthlessness and insistence |
| Sagittarius | Nov. 23–Dec. 21, 23 | Fairness and propriety |
| Capricorn | Dec. 22, 24–Jan. 20 | Stubbornness and independence |
| Aquarius | Jan. 21–Feb. 19 | Conviction and cleverness |
| Pisces | Feb. 20–March 20 | Tolerance and compassion |

# Ruling Planets

Each one of these signs is ruled by a planet named for a mythological god, including Venus, Mars, Mercury, Jupiter, Saturn, Uranus, Neptune, and Pluto. In astrological terms, the sun and the moon are also considered planets. The planets all have inherent traits that must be considered when doing any kind of astrological magick. And those influences need to be considered in conjunction with the sign to explain the astrological significance. Following are the major "business" traits *Corporate Magick* has identified for each planet:

| Planet | Business Trait |
| --- | --- |
| Sun | Masculine management |
| Moon | Change |
| Mercury | Intelligence |
| Venus | Love of career |

| Planet | Business Trait |
| --- | --- |
| Mars | Conflict, aggression |
| Jupiter | Growth |
| Saturn | Inhibition |
| Uranus | Creativity |
| Neptune | Stealth |
| Pluto | Power |

# The 12 Houses and Their Personal Effects

Another important piece to the astrological puzzle is the ascending (rising in the east) "houses." There are twelve planetary houses (divided into twelve thirty-degree sectors of the horoscope). For each zodiac sign there is a corresponding house, but unlike the zodiac signs that revolve around the skies, the houses are fixed sections on the horoscope chart. When a planet passes through a house, that's how you determine the sign. Keep in mind that houses really give information on everyday life—the "Departments of Life"—so the business aspects of houses relate more to individuals in companies than the companies themselves.

| House | Effect |
| --- | --- |
| First house | Assertiveness |
| Second house | Conservatism and possessions |
| Third house | Communication |
| Fourth house | Security |
| Fifth house | Creativity |
| Sixth house | Work |
| Seventh house | Partnerships |
| Eighth house | Money and investments |
| Ninth house | Information and law |
| Tenth house | Ambition and career |
| Eleventh house | Politics |
| Twelfth house | Service |

# Elements and Aspects

The elements, earth, wind, air, and fire, are always held in high regard in magick, often being represented in rituals and ceremonies. It is held by many sorcerers that if you can control the elements, then you control the very world around you. And so it is true with astrology. The twelve zodiac signs are also related to the four elements, as follows: earth (Virgo, Taurus, Capricorn); air (Gemini, Libra, Aquarius); fire (Aries, Leo, Sagittarius); and water (Cancer, Scorpio, Pisces). They are referred to in these relations as "triplicities" (three signs to each element). Each sign also has either cardinal, fixed, or mutable traits. Cardinal traits represent initiative; fixed traits are steadfast; and mutable traits are changeable. Four zodiac signs, or the "quadrupities," are assigned to each of these qualities. In addition, there are five major planetary aspects or influences that astrologers must take into consideration. They are conjunction, which can be positive or negative; opposition and square, which are negative; and trine and sextile, which are both positive.

The days of the week and how they're connected with the ruling planets also play a role in successful star charting, especially when doing spell casting. So when you're working magick, consider the day to be an important piece of the puzzle.

I know this is confusing stuff, and you're probably asking if it's really necessary. Well, it is when doing serious astrological readings, but it's commonly understood that the elements and the quadrupities combined give the most accurate indication of a sign's true nature. And I've combined all of them with the other "influences" in a master chart that follows, which you can consult for quick information. The most important part of the master chart is the "Business Quality" area, which takes into account a number of astrological pieces including the planets, the four elements, the houses, male/female, positive/negative qualities, days of the week, and more so that you can use a simplified chart that delivers a solid business profile for that sign. When in doubt, consult this part of the chart first.

# Chart Youself

Remember, a very important aspect of using astrology in the
*Corporate Magick* system is knowing your own sign and its traits
and influences. The most crucial thing to consider is your time of
birth (exact time is often "fudged" in something called rectification, which allows for a number of different birth times). So be
sure of your house with its particular attributes. For example, the
second house deals with money and possessions, and the tenth
house has to do with career, both of which will become important to you, the corporate magician. When charting yourself, consult the special tables called "Ephemerides," (published yearly by
Raphael of London), which locate the positions of signs and
planets on the eastern horizon at the time and place of birth. The
point where your eastern horizon intersected your sign on the
zodiac is called the "ascendant"—an important part of the charting process. So, for example, corporate magicians with their signs
and ruling planet ascending in the second or tenth houses would
most likely be in an advantageous position for business success.

It is also important to know the compatibility factors of the
person or company involved in your magick. We can fill volumes
with listings and comparison charts as to what sign jives better
with what other sign. So rely on the *Corporate Magick* Master
Astrology Table (see page 85) and use some common sense. For
example, if a person's element is fire and yours is water . . . well,
you get the picture. And if that sounds too simplistic, you'll find
that with further in-depth study of astrology, most are simple
logical conclusions.

# The Method

*Corporate Magick* uses a combination of traditional magick and
astrology. I've combined information from both disciplines and
blended them into a system that works for those interested in
getting some magickal help without becoming full-blown astrologers. Now that you're prepared with the tools of the as-

trologer, you can begin working magick with the help of the zodiac. Remember that we are using the basic intelligence offered from the zodiac signs, their ruling planets, the elements, and how they all interact and influence reality.

*Corporate Magick* is unique because it doesn't subscribe to the orthodox methods of horoscope reading. Your goal is to understand the relationship of the stars to your magickal workings. As we've already learned, this system uses all and any magickal means to an end. And that end is always success. So if you're concerned with an individual, then discover his sign, its house, and any other pertinent astrological information, such as actual time and day of birth, on what cusp of the zodiac was his house, and so on. This can all be ascertained by consulting the "Ephemerides" manuals. And likewise, if it's a company you are concerned with, find out when the company was formed, what signs the executives are under, and any other factors that will effect your magick. Marcus Goodwin states in his book that stocks have lives. "Stocks are like people. They really are . . . Each stock is born, lives for a while, and dies, as people do. All are in synchronicity with the biological rhythms and cycles of our gracious creator. As with the stars, stocks are in harmony with the universe or in some cases, at dissonance with it." So it is with a company . . . find out its life cycle and work the magick.

## *Corporate Magick* Master Astrology Table

| Sign | Ruling Planet | Business Quality | M/F Trait | Element | Spell Day |
|------|---------------|------------------|-----------|---------|-----------|
| Aries | Mars | Leadership | Masc. | Fire | Tuesday |
| Taurus | Venus | Security | Fem. | Earth | Friday |
| Gemini | Mercury | Strategy | Masc. | Air | Wednesday |
| Cancer | Moon | Political | Fem. | Water | Monday |
| Leo | Sun | Executive | Masc. | Fire | Sunday |
| Virgo | Mercury | Management | Fem. | Earth | Wednesday |
| Libra | Venus | Partnerships | Masc. | Air | Friday |
| Scorpio | Mars | Finances | Fem. | Water | Tuesday |
| Sagittarius | Jupiter | Legal | Masc. | Fire | Thursday |
| Capricorn | Saturn | Accounting | Fem. | Earth | Saturday |

| Sign | Ruling Planet | Business Quality | M/F Trait | Element | Spell Day |
|------|---------------|------------------|-----------|---------|-----------|
| Aquarius | Uranus | Creative | Masc. | Air | Thursday |
| Pisces | Neptune | Supervisor | Fem. | Water | Tuesday |

Key: Masc. = aggressive, fixed, take charge. Fem. = passive, changeable, adaptable. Fire = spiritive, impulsive. Earth = practical, dependable. Air = Stealth, expressive. Water = intuitive, negotiator.

### *Corporate Magick* Quick Astrology Reference Chart

Use this chart when you need to match a person or a company within a certain industry quickly to their astrological sign, or if you're considering an investment. Of course there will be multiple combinations that can apply, but this is a solid starting point for your magick. Remember to use the signs in conjunction with other magickal spells and rituals for the *Corporate Magick* way.

| Personnel | Signs That Fit Best |
|-----------|---------------------|
| CEOs | Leo, Virgo |
| Senior Executives | Aries, Leo, Pisces, Virgo |
| Managers | Virgo, Pisces, Libra |
| Financial | Scorpio, Sagittarius, Taurus |
| Legal | Sagittarius, Capricorn |
| Marketing /advertising | Aquarius, Virgo |
| Communications | Aquarius, Cancer |
| Sales | Scorpio, Capricorn, Libra |
| Administrative | Pisces, Taurus, Scorpio |

| Industries | When Company Started or Initial Public Offering (IPO) |
|------------|-------------------------------------------------------|
| Financial | Taurus |
| Entertainment | Aquarius, Gemini |
| Manufacturing | Virgo |
| Consulting | Leo |
| Internet | Virgo, Aries |

| Industries | When Company Started or Initial Public Offering (IPO) |
|---|---|
| Media | Aquarius |
| Law | Sagittarius |
| Services | Cancer |

---

## CASE STUDY
## DIANA'S DATES

While recently having my house painted, my designer, Diana, a staunch believer and a fanatical horoscope buff, and I had a long conversation about the zodiac and how she has consulted the stars since she was a teenager. She recounted numerous stories about how she'd discovered who was going to escort her to her senior prom, how much she should pay for her new car, what her sister was thinking some three thousand miles away, and many, many more interesting life tales. Diana told me that she believed wholeheartedly that her sign was true to her real personality, and even when she thought her readings were off, after some time she realized that she "grew" into their descriptions. In effect, the zodiac was not only advising, but actually predicting Diana's future.

But when our conversation turned to her business, Diana's demeanor quickly soured. She said that she just wasn't getting the amount of business she was used to and that she and her two partners were not getting along. Diana was facing tough times and lamented that she didn't know how to turn things around.

I told Diana that as a lifelong student of astrology, she should use the stars for help. She'd never considered the horoscope as a business adviser because she was conditioned to think it was geared only toward personal areas of life. Diana knew that the daily readings often mentioned career choices and opportune times for approaching the boss, but she'd never made the connection that astrology could assist in larger business dealings as well. Until we talked about *Corporate Magick* and knowing the difference between simply reading your chart and being reactive, and knowing how your stars will *interact* with other people and businesses, and being proactive. That's the key to the method—

use the stars as a guide, use the information at hand, and then perform the magick to make it all work. The corporate magician blends the two disciplines—astrology and magick—in a magickal one–two punch.

I asked Diana what her biggest business problem was at the moment, and she revealed that it was the animosity with her partners. "Our signs just don't mix and match . . . that's the problem," she told me. I said that it might be a problem, but it was also valuable information. I instructed Diana to find out as much as she could about the partners' signs in a casual and friendly manner, and to also learn how much they believed in the stars (again, the belief—on both ends—assists the magick).

Once she knew her partners' astrological profiles, she could work some magick. "I found out that my main partner was a Capricorn and ruled by the planet Saturn, a planet that caused her to have a very restrictive mind-set. She was often negative—another aspect of her sign—so the combination was debilitating for our business," Diana said. But Capricorns' quadrupity is "cardinal," which means they take initiative. After we discussed the matter at length, Diana deduced that her partner needed to take on less of the business's paperwork (easing her restrictive nature) and increase her field sales work to seek new business (more initiative).

Diana conducted a simple ritual one evening using an onyx stone (a gem associated with Saturn, her partner's ruling planet), and sent the message of a new working relationship between the two into the ethereal plane. The spell worked. After a long talk, Diana's partner was elated that she could "redirect" her energies. Her negativity dissipated, and Diana's business was back in swing.

---

# The Age of Aquarius

Much has been said in the world of astrology in the last thirty years concerning the Age of Aquarius and its impact on the stars and life in general. Truth be told, astrologers don't even agree if the Age of Aquarius—the first new age in two thousand years—has actually begun yet. Most agree that we are just entering Aquarius and leaving the age of Pisces—a rather restrictive and sullen age—that will culminate about one hundred years from now. So you are witnessing the birth of the Aquarian Age, with its promise of high spirituality, hope, and, interestingly enough, an increase in the occult arts. It is an obviously opportune time to use magick. The Aquarian air sign rules electricity and aeronautics and radioactive elements, so it might be a good time to delve into those industries. And advances in ESP and psychic research will yield astounding breakthroughs aided by new technologies. So your future as a corporate magician is bright. Work your magick.

## INSTANT MAGICK INDEX CARD

### Astrological Spell Casting

1. Gather as much pertinent astrological information (birth dates, time of birth, past belief in astrology) on the individual or company to receive your magick as you can.
2. Know your own sign and all of its influences.
3. Consult the *Corporate Magick* Master Astrology Table.
4. Cross-reference how your sign interacts with your magickal target's sign.

# CHAPTER 6

# Voodoo—Get Your *Mojo* Working

There are probably times that you wish you had a voodoo doll that you could stick pins into and wreak vengeance on a business rival. You envision your nemesis experiencing all kinds of physical and mental pain in your effort to wield some magickal justice. Can you picture it? Your jackass of a boss gives you a hard time for no good reason and embarrasses you in front of the entire office. You run back to your desk, grab a poppet doll made in his likeness—fat gut and all—and then jab a pin right in its side. Then there the boss goes, running out of his office and holding his side in agony like the coward he is, while you secretly chuckle in your office.

I'm sure that this scenario played out at least one time in your imagination, or at least something similar. I'm also sure that at some time in your business career, you were tempted to actually buy a novelty voodoo doll (under the guise of pure fun, of course) that came equipped with pins and sectioned diagrams of where to stick them for maximum effectivencss. "Hey, if I buy a voodoo doll and stick some pins in it, I get revenge, quick and easy," you fantasized.

Well, let's set the record straight both for the world of magick and how *Corporate Magick* deals with the occult world's most colorful and diverse magickal system. We'll start with the obvious. Voodoo dolls and all of the media hype, legends, horror movies, and so called "voodoo priests" who sell voodoo wares on the Internet are fun. But none of the typical voodoo "hoodoo" will work real magick unless you, the magician, understand what's behind this powerful system and are able to tap into its mysteries. Fortunately, what you now hold in your hands is the real deal for using voodoo—or more properly referred to in occult circles as "Voudon," a pseudo-magickal religion born in Africa and ultimately transported to the island of Haiti with the slave trade. Voodoo, in fact, is far more a religion steeped in tradition and ancestral legends and beliefs than it is a magickal system. But because this book deals with getting you what you need accomplished in the business world, the *Corporate Magick* brand of voodoo is customized and made practical whether you are an aspiring *oungan* (priest), *mambo* (priestess), or full-fledged *boko* (voodoo sorcerer).

An important aspect of voodoo that you must keep in mind is that the religion's practitioners believe that the supernatural is a negative force—a disease—that must be polarized and then used for good. The *oungans* and *mambos* traditionally will not perform magick for self-gain or material gain, but are more healers and oracles. They have a love–hate relationship with the pantheon of supernatural beings, sacrificing food and often animals to their gods on one hand and fearing them as demons who can wreak havoc on their lives on the other. Much of the system's ceremony and ritual revolve around these powerful supernatural spirits called *loas* or *mysteres* who are collectively referred to as "the invisibles."

Often, those who have dabbled in voodoo erroneously believe that practitioners also worship the Roman Catholic saints, but the truth is that saints' pictures are just representations to camouflage the actual voodoo gods. When colonists from France and Spain forced African slaves in Haiti to accept Catholicism in the late seventeenth century, the newly "baptized" were forced to practice their traditional folk religions in secrecy. Coupled with the native faiths of Haiti, the underground slave religion developed into the amalgamation of beliefs that grew into the mysterious religion we know as voodoo—the spirit of the unknown.

Our modern interpretation of voodoo, complete with zombies, possessions, *mojo* bags, and other "pop" icons, developed because of the religion's fascinatingly diverse mixture of music, wild rituals, colorful talismans, food and animal sacrifices, and, of course, its mysterious relationship with the dead and the supernatural. And it's this very macabre symbolism that makes voodoo such a powerful magickal system, because it invokes so many emotional responses in practitioners and believers alike. Through these symbols, which range from pictures to flat stones adorned with bits of broken mirror (thunderstones) to *gris-gris* bags, the magician's power becomes enhanced and more focused.

Voodoo is the "bastard child" of *Corporate Magick* because for practical purposes we are extracting its magickal function, and, for the most part, not dealing with its religious core. We will be concentrating on its symbolism—the magickal aspects of voodoo's power—to create useful tools. Think of the symbolic side of voodoo as you would any other religion. In Catholicism, the likeness of St. Anthony is displayed and prayed to when believers are faced with the impossible. In Judaism a *mezuzah* (usually a representation of biblical scrolls) inscribed with the name of God is placed on the front door of a home or apartment to bring good fortune. All religions have symbolic fetishes that evoke strong emotions and act as a conduit for divine help, but most don't describe the act as "magick." Voodoo, on the other hand, freely uses its magickal symbolism in its religious ceremonies, albeit in a much more hedonistic, colorful, and "ghostly" manner, relying much more on the spirit world of the dead. *Corporate Magick*'s approach to using voodoo is to take this potent symbolism, customize its effect on physical items, and construct portable, instant, and easy-to-use magickal devices for almost any business situation, without requiring the magician to adhere to voodoo's traditional belief system.

The traditional approach of working voodoo magick, usually only conducted by the *oungan, mambo,* or *boko,* is to call on the pantheon of deities in ceremony. The voodoo "officials" are the only people within the society empowered to manipulate what's believed to be the malevolent supernatural for good, whether it be to create a healing powder or protective charm, or used in a full-blown ritual in which someone is possessed by the spirit of a *loa*. But as a corporate magician, you have already been initiated in the ways of the mage (see chapter 2 on preparation), so by readying yourself for magick you will be open to receiving any and all universal energy to perform your magick regardless of the discipline. In addition, by practicing the three basic steps and six statements every day, you'll be getting yourself in powerful magickal condition.

And by recognizing the inherent powers of the *loas* and knowing their effects on the material world for each voodoo symbol you create, your thoughts—transferred as energy—will create the magick to work in whichever implement you use. As in all magick, it is your very will and thought-energies that act as the magickal engine. It doesn't really matter what system you are working within; they will all respond if your mind accepts, believes, and focuses its power. Each magickal tool you forge through voodoo practice will absorb the energy of the gods and spirits.

There are a number of charms and spells used in voodoo for various scenarios, from protection to cursing an enemy. Each contains myriad ingredients, including herbs, pieces of bone, food, oils, and even hair and fingernail clippings. The ingredients can be contained in bags, bottles, or lamps; sewn into clothing; and even used in baths, depending on the desired outcome and what deity or spirit is being conjured. But the preparations for these charms are far from simple, and they must be made in the presence of a priest or priestess. For example, to protect against an enemy, a "black lamp" is created and offered to the *loa* Agwe.* The "lamp" is made of pumpkin, bones, powdered lizard, castor oil, hot pepper, and more. The ingredients are refilled for seven weeks and then tossed into Agwe's ocean king-

*From *The Book of Voudou*, by Leah Gordon.

dom to satiate his hunger and make the magick happen. True believers don't expect a literal and instantaneous answer from the spirits, but instead realize the outcome over the normal course of events in their lives. So if you create a black lamp, you may not see your enemy disappear, but the animosity between you and your rival may dissipate over time.

---

## CASE STUDY
## PAF, A REAL VOODOO "DOLL"

---

My good friend Paf, a successful Internet entrepreneur, has been fascinated with the Haitian culture and especially its magickal beliefs since she spent some time in the country as a child. Her parents, who were professors doing anthropological grant studies for a major university in southern California, often explained to Paf that voodoo was much more than a set of superstitious rules; it was in fact a very integral part of the everyday lives of the natives. The young girl began to study voodoo and its magick on a daily basis, and after some time was as proficient in its use as the locals. Her love of voodoo among her peers at that time, and her firsthand witness of its results, gave Paf a life-long respect for the workings of the customs and practices. She often used voodoo charms to get her through tough times, and she credits the art with helping her become one of the Internet's leading providers of large-sized women's clothes.

One of her most difficult business challenges really put Paf's faith in voodoo to the test. When at first blush she mentioned that she often used the magick of the Islands to help her in her career, and in this time of crisis was going to call on the spirits once again, her associates cringed and responded with reactions like, "Isn't voodoo all about zombies and wild orgies?" But once Paf explained her beliefs in the charms she had been given throughout her life and the positive results they always yielded, the naysayers stopped and listened.

And at this time Paf needed to prove a lot more than her faith in voodoo. She suspected that she was being swindled by a partner and realized that she needed help from the spirits to reveal the culprit and also to protect her small company. Paf knew that the money flowing into her fledgling business was healthy—not millions, but impressive for a small Web site nevertheless. However, she couldn't understand why bills weren't being met and why her subcontractors weren't being paid. She saw the books on a regular basis and she knew the checks were being cut; yet her suppliers were up in arms.

An old *mambo* from Paf's days in Haiti once provided her father with a special *juju* (good-luck charm) *gris-gris* bag when a conspiring academic colleague tried to prove her father wasn't worthy of his university grant. The magickal bag was made from a piece of flannel cloth and filled with African gingerroot, basil leaves, bay leaves, and mandrake root—herbs all known to protect from evil. Paf recalled how her dad humored the *mambo* at first, not really believing in the power of magickal charms, but after things started to turn in his favor and his accuser was exposed for fraud himself, the little flannel bag took on quite a bit more importance in Paf's family's life. In fact, her father gave Paf the bag to keep with her as a good-luck memento of their happy times in Haiti.

It wasn't until Paf was faced with her most stealthy adversary that she recalled the *gris-gris* bag and how it had helped her dad. She rummaged through her closet until she found the bag, determined to let it do its magick once again and expose her untrustworthy partner. "I was literally brought back to the time as a child in Haiti, and I could hear the drumbeat that often lulled me to sleep at night," Paf recalled. "I knew the *oungans* and *mambos* were practicing great magick those nights, and I hoped that this little bag I held in my hands once again retained some of the power that aided my dad."

What may have looked like a card table full of colored props, sweets, and dolls was actually Paf's altar dedicated to the spirit Danbhala, who is known to impart wisdom. But the most bizarre objects noticed by the uninitiated were eggs—a favorite offering to Danbhala. Each spirit has a list of associated offerings, colors, among others. As you continue your exploration into magick you'll see how related most disciplines really are, sharing common practices and using sympathetic magick in most areas of spell casting and creating talismans and charms.

Armed with her old *gris-gris* bag and using magickal prowess learned many years before, Paf conducted a simple ceremony each night for one week asking Danbhala to expose any wrongdoing in her company and to have the culprit expelled. In true voodoo fashion, there was no bolt of lightning that hit her larcenous partner . . . but a bounced check gave him up. It seems he was writing checks to his girlfriend from the company's funds. When one of the checks was written for an amount higher than Paf's balance, the check was returned to her. Paf noticed that the name on the check wasn't a client, and her partner was busted. Danbhala did his job; the *gris-gris* bag was put away for future consultation, and Paf's faith in the power of voodoo—*in business*—was kept strong.

---

# The *Loas*

The *loas* are the spirit gods of voodoo and the magickal supervisors who make it all happen. Voodoo practitioners ask the *loas* for help and favors by offering food and, sometimes, animal sacrifices. *Loas* communicate with the spirit world, visit the earth, and possess human souls through ceremony by voodoo priests. The relationship between the mortal and the *loa* in voodoo is a very special bonding. The magician must serve the *loa* by offering various sacrifices, but the relationship is usually built over a lifetime. And what makes it most interesting to *Corporate Magick* is that this close-knit friendship with the guardian spirit, called a *"met tet"*—roughly translated as "the *loa* sitting on your head"—is based on what the *loa* commands and its advantage for the believer. Farmers worship Zaka, lord of agriculture; cops worship Ayza, whose domain is protection; and so forth.

In *Corporate Magick,* you will be using a similar method of identifying the *loa* who can help in your specific industry; then you will use other devices in combination to reach your goals. For example, Agwe is the god of the oceans, so he would influence any marine or fishing industry. In conjunction with a *gris-gris* bag containing the proper ingredients, or other implement, you can create a powerful magickal business aid.

To satisfy the *loa,* you will provide offerings that fit with tradition; however, you will also provide offerings that are accessible to you. So you won't be offering animal sacrifices (for many reasons besides practicality), but you may offer a "sympathetic" representation of an animal the *loa* desires. Because there are numerous "gifts" and sacrifices for each *loa,* and there are many, many more *loas* in different voodoo sect pantheons than are listed on page 98, *Corporate Magick* makes using the spirits' power simple.

## How to Use Voodoo at Work

Once you have prepared yourself for magick using the methods in chapter 2, you can then begin using the power of voodoo in business. I have broken down each *loa's* influence and listed the charms, lamps, thunderstones, and dolls that will work in conjunction with that loa, as well as what each implement is best used for. As a corporate magician, all you need to do to make voodoo magick is follow these simple steps (or use the Instant Magick Index Card at the end of this chapter):

1. Choose the business situation you want to influence.
2. Create the magickal implement for the particular scenario.
3. Make an offering to the affiliated *loa.*
4. Visualize the outcome of your magick.

If you don't already have an altar built for your other magickal workings, you should have one in order to work the voodoo magick. Representations of the *loa* need to be somewhere physical so you can make an offering to the spirit while you are in your magickal (focused and meditative) state of mind, ready to unleash your energy. In addition, you will need a place to prepare and add the ingredients in your charms and other voodoo tools. The altar does not have to be elaborate; it can be your desk, a table, or a mantel. Just be sure it is within a private area, and that you have at least purified the area with your favorite incense. Once you're prepared, you will be ready for *la prise des yeux*— "the taking hold of the eyes," or the gift of spiritual power.

*Loas* are traditionally "called" during a voodoo ceremony with a *veve,* a symbol drawn in flour on the ground of the voodoo temple. This is similar to other magickal sigils and talismans that are the supernatural calling cards used to summon spirits, gods, and demons alike. In *Corporate Magick*, the magician's innate will is a more powerful summoning device than a mere drawing, so we rely more on mental prowess than artistic ability.

# The Major *Loas* and the Industries They Influence

| Spirit | Dominion | Industry |
|---|---|---|
| Agwe | Oceans | Marine, fishing, cruises |
| Aida Wedo | The sky | Airlines, weather |
| Ayza | Protection | Law, security, safety |
| Baron Samedi | Death | Funeral, cemetery |
| Danbhala | Wisdom | Information, computers |
| Ezili | Love and beauty | Fashion, cosmetics |
| Mawu Lisa | Creation | Arts, media |
| Marasa | Partnering | Medicine |
| Ogou | Healing | Medicine, fitness |
| Papa Legba | Gatekeeper | Finance, insurance |
| Zaka | Agriculture | Farming, forestry |

## Offerings to the Major *Loas*

| Spirit | Offerings |
|---|---|
| Agwe | Chicken, champagne, cake |
| Aida Wedo | Eggs, rice, olive oil, liqueur |
| Ayza | Rooster feathers |
| Baron Samedi | Peanuts, coffee, rum |
| Danbhala | Flowers, eggs, fruit, cake |
| Ezili | Sweets, perfume, pork |
| Mawu Lisa | Perfume |
| Marasa | Toys, fizzy drinks, popcorn |
| Ogou | Rice, cigars, red beans |
| Papa Legba | Smoked meats, tobacco, yams |
| Zaka | Corn, sugarcane, rice |

# Voodoo Charms

There are three types of voodoo charms that have their roots in New Orleans voodoo—a more Americanized brand of the magick—which we will be working with in *Corporate Magick* because they best serve us in our business concerns. They are: the *juju, gris-gris,* and *mojo.* Keep in mind that these charms take many different forms in the voodoo world, from bags to bottles, and the word "charm" is merely a catchall referring to their magickal ability.

The *juju* is primarily a "white magick" charm made for luck and to attract love, fortune, and friendship. The *gris-gris* (loosely translated to "gray" or between white and black, positive and negative) is the most powerful, but is more of an all-purpose charm that can be used for a variety of wishes, from simple good luck to causing physical harm. And the *mojo,* with a strong relation to *mo* or the spirits of the dead, are considered the "black magick" charms made expressly for defense, harm, and retribution.

A fourth charm is the *paket Kongo,* a piece of satin cloth wrapped as a packet, knotted seven times, and adorned with ribbons, gems, horns, sparkles, and other colorful items most commonly used for protection. The *paket Kongo*'s ingredients usually include herbs and powders directly related to the *loa* that's to receive the offering. It is said that the spirit's power will reside in the *paket Kongo* and remain there for seven years.

Other charms used for voodoo include *loa* lamps and bottles, thunderstones, and voodoo dolls.

Each one of these charms has been identified to work best with specific areas of business and the workplace. After you have created the charm and made the offering to your selected *loa* spirit, place the charm in the area you want the magick to work or carry it on your person (if possible).

What follows are the charms you need to create specific business results, along with the necessary ingredients (most oils and powders can be found in local occult shops or *botanicas* that specialize in Afro-Caribbean religious articles and herbs (see Appendix: Resources).

## The Juju
### *(use for Raises, Promotions, Partnerships, Sales)*

Secure a small leather pouch, rub in money-drawing oil, and add buckeye root, rattlesnake root, silver coins, and a business card of a friend or associate who has a title you seek or who is your desired partner. Burn a copy of your most recent resumé over a green candle. Collect the ashes and mix them in with the other *juju* ingredients. Then select the *loa* of your industry, place the *juju* on your altar, and make the offering while in your magickal state of mind.

## The Gris-Gris
### *(use for Meetings, Presentations, Loans, Personnel, Negotiations)*

Find a piece of red flannel cloth that you can make into a pouch or bag. Fill the bag with mandrake root, St. John the Conqueror root, an eagle feather, and an object from the place in which the meeting or presentation will occur (if you have access). If not, include something from the company or person (a page from an annual report, letterhead). (Ideally, if you have fingernails or a strand of hair from the person you are trying to influence, this will make the *gris-gris* that much more powerful.) Sprinkle the ingredients with cinnamon (the total must be an odd number no more than thirteen).

   *Note:* It is advisable when using herbs in a *gris-gris* that you test them to determine if the herbs agree with your magickal being. You can do this by holding the herb in your hands and concentrating. If you feel a strange vibration of any kind—a tingle of sorts—this means the power works with you. If you feel nothing, the herb may not be in harmony with you and you should use some other herb with similar properties. Make your offering to your *loa* and then wear the *gris-gris* on your person at the time and place of your business meeting.

## *The* Mojo
*(use for Defense, Competition, Counterintelligence)*

Considered the most "negative" of the voodoo charms, the *mojo* is, in fact, a strong charm for providing protection and defense in the *Corporate Magick* system when its power is directed at someone who is bent on doing you harm. To prepare your *mojo*, use a leather pouch. On a square piece of paper, write the name of the person whom you are defending yourself against nine times. Fold the corners of the paper inward into a diamond shape and rub the paper with four thieves vinegar. Obtain a piece of beeswax and roll into a ball. Drop flying devil's oil into the center of the ball and seal it, preferably along with fingernail clippings or hair of your intended magickal rival. Melt the wax onto the paper, sealing the corners. Then make your offering to your *loa* and place the *mojo* in an area that your rival is known to frequent.

## *The* Paket Kongo
*(use for Business Longevity, Long-term Projects and Goals)*

Usually made for protection, the *paket Kongo* is said to bind the *loa* to your wishes for seven years, so it should be used for long-range goals. Use a piece of colored satin cloth (usually the color of the *loa* you're asking to help) that corresponds to your industry:

Marine and airline—white and blue
Law—blue and red
Funeral—black and purple
Fashion and beauty—pink
Information—white
Arts and media—blue and green
Medicine and fitness—red
Finance—red and white
Agriculture—blue and red

Include items of your business—papers, photos—in multiples of seven. Include mandrake root, garlic powder, frankincense, and the feather of a rooster. Bind the cloth into an onion-shaped pouch with a ribbon and tie the knot seven times. Attach something of importance to your business on the top of the pouch. Under a full moon, place the pouch on your altar and make the offering to your *loa*. Place the *paket* at the entrance of your business or carry it in your briefcase.

## Loa *Lamps and Bottles*
### *(use for Major Business Problems)*

*Loa* lamps and bottles are created to establish immediate aid from the *loa* that continues on a daily basis. Both the lamp and the bottle can use the same ingredients; however, the bottle is usually "agitated" into working more quickly by lashing it.

To make a lamp, use a bowl, cup, or coconut shell filled with oil. String a wick through the bowl and secure it with pieces of bone splinter on both sides of the hole. Add alfalfa, mustard seeds, castor oil, mandrake root, and soil from a crossroads (or cemetery, if the lamp is to deflect an attack). Add a symbolic representation of the business problem (write down the problem or use a negative bank statement or legal document) and tear it into small pieces into the oil. Light the wick and make the offering to the *loa* on your altar. Place the lamp at your business or at your workplace and light the lamp each day until the oil is used up.

The *loa* bottle can contain the same ingredients, but it must be corked and then suspended after a full day of burning. Once it is corked, hang it outdoors and whip it with a lash made of leather to "excite" the *loa* into action.

## *Thunderstones*
### *(use for Sudden Tasks)*

The small, flat oval stones adorned with pieces of mirror called "thunderstones" are instant charms in that they can be easily carried and used for "quick fixes." According to legend, the talismans originated at the beginning of time when the gods hurled fragments of creation at earth. And according to voodoo tradition, the thunderstones are passed down through the generations to amplify the practitioner's magickal abilities. So technically speaking, you can't create them.

However, I believe we can create thunderstones by virtue of infusing them with the *loa* spirit just as we do any charm. Choose some small, flat stonelike object, adorn it with any glitter you choose (best if it represents your line of work), and offer it to your *loa* at your altar. Carry it in all business situations and hold it in your hand, when you can, to draw on its energy. The thunderstone in effect, becomes your portable *Corporate Magick* magick battery.

### The Voodoo Doll
*(use for All Purposes)*

Last but not least is the somewhat mythical voodoo charm commonly called the "voodoo doll." The authentic use of the doll is actually as a "messenger doll"—a hand-sewn cloth doll that delivers the practitioner's wishes to the *loa*. Dolls are also used to adorn voodoo altars to please the *loas*. Messenger dolls can serve both purposes after they "deliver" their message.

The simplest of the charms, you can make the messenger doll out of cloth or purchase one at an occult or New Age shop. If a plain doll with no features is not available, a "standard" voodoo doll will do in the *Corporate Magick* system because, as I've stated, your will is more important than the vehicle. Once you have the doll, write down your wishes on a piece of paper and tie it to the doll with the colored ribbon of the *loa* of your industry (see page 98). Leave the doll at a crossroads or in a cemetery.

And if the notion strikes you and you just can't resist, make a voodoo doll (really a poppet) in the likeness of someone who has done you wrong, jab it with pins, and maybe you'll feel better. But remember: The real magick is not in the doll, it's in *you*.

## INSTANT MAGICK INDEX CARD

### How to Make a Voodoo Charm

Use a green pouch (or a piece of green cloth that can be folded into a pouch); add coins, soil, cinnamon, and a piece of paper with your desires written on it.

Wrap the contents together in pouch form; tie it with a red ribbon.

Make an offering of a white bird feather to Simbi, the patron saint of voodoo magick.

Call on the *Corporate Magick* Cabal to deliver the message to Simbi.

## CHAPTER 7

# Santeria for Success

Santeria, an Afro-Caribbean magickal system that's often affectionately referred to as "natural" or "jungle magick" because of its heavy use of organic materials including herbs, powders, soil, and the sacrifice of live animals, is a first cousin to voodoo in many ways. Both systems worship a pantheon of gods. In Santeria the gods are called *orishas,* who are the supreme being Olodunare's emissaries here on earth. Good spirits to know when you need something done in the business world.

Even more so than voodoo, Santeria relies heavily on Roman Catholic influence, particularly the use of saints. Its also known for wild possessions and lusty drum beating, which are part of the religion's ritualistic psychodrama. A major difference lies in the perception of each practice, however. Whereas voodoo refers to its use of magick as white, black, and even "gray," Santeria claims its magick is exclusively "white" and performed only for good. This "spin" has much to do with the system's origins and use of Roman Catholic saints. What makes Santeria most interesting to users of *Corporate Magick* is that although the *santero,* (male) or *santera* (female) priests profess to perform only positive magick, they do have the option of doing some serious harm if the magick is used for defense against or retribution for some heinous act. If you recall, this, too, is a major tenet of *Corporate Magick*. Magick *can* and should be used against a less-than-scrupulous business acquaintance if he is attempting to do you harm. As you will see, Santeria's spells fit nicely with our bottom-line approach to the world of magick.

Because Santeria's magick is so dependent on thousands of mixtures of organic materials and special natural items like the *palos* (special tree sticks that wield awesome magickal powers when correctly used), trying to break down ingredients into a useful, pragmatic methodology would be daunting to our goals. This bothersome combination of animal sacrifice and the syncretistic association with Catholic saints makes Santeria a magickal system that is better for the corporate magician to use with ready-made spells than to try to master as a discipline. What's more, because each god, or *orisha,* is so tied in with Catholicism, literally using the saints and their images as "front men" for ceremony may turn off some corporate magicians who are not inclined to accept Catholicism.

That being said, Santeria is a very effective method of achieving material goals. But I have treated the presentation of the "natural arts" of Santeria in the *Corporate Magick* system differently. I have included actual case studies of associates, friends, and colleagues whom I have interviewed, particularly from the areas of Miami and New York (two strongholds of Santeria tradition), who are either practitioners of Santeria or, because of family influence, have used the spells and charms handed down through the generations. These people are all business professionals who may not completely understand the philosophy and magickal zeitgeist of Santeria, but they know it works! You will still be able to use and apply the magickal spells and techniques by referring to the examples that follow each case study. Each example points out the *orisha* who was called upon for help in a particular business challenge and how the spell was facilitated. And at the end of each story, the spell's ingredients are listed so that you, the corporate magician, can simply copy the spell and use it for your own needs.

As you read the case studies you'll see that each scenario has a connection to one of seven *orishas*—Elleggua, Obatala, Chango, Oggun, Orunla, Yemaya, and Oshun—the seven high deities in the Santeria pantheon commonly referred to as the "Seven African Powers." The *orishas* are another reason Santeria is appealing: They are the spirits whom humans deal with directly for help—a practical approach that fits well with *Corporate Magick*'s pragmatic philosophy.

The spells that will follow include the devotions and offerings that are necessary. Almost all of the ingredients can be found at a local *botanica* (Spanish occult supply store) or on the Internet (see Appendix: Resources).

# *Orisha* Elleggua (The Divine Messenger)

## *Carlos's Goal: Managing a Staff Long Distance*

For hundreds of years, Cuban cigars have been the premier smoking experience for cigar lovers the world over. And since the United States levied its trade embargo on Cuba, the cigar-smoking public was forced to look elsewhere for their tobacco pleasures, particularly Nicaragua and the Dominican Republic. This created quite a business challenge for Carlos, a vice president of sales and marketing for a major tobacco company based in the Dominican Republic, which had experienced astounding growth and demand in the early to mid 1990s when a cigar-smoking craze swept across America among young well-to-do business types.

The buying public couldn't get enough of Carlos's product. His operation expanded at an astounding 150 percent growth rate, and with this came an ever-increasing responsibility to be able to manage efficiently and meet the market demands. What was most disturbing to the young vice president was that he was based in Miami and his company's headquarters, with all of the corporate honchos, was in South America. When he began with the company, he had no problem directing his small sales force of five people, who traveled across the continental United States selling their product. But when the cigar boom hit, his staff became a small army; Carlos became hard-pressed to manage his own time, much less the intricate schedules, sales meetings, and corporate directives added to his list of daily duties.

As the demand for the Dominican cigars grew, Carlos became more and more frazzled and worried that he could no longer handle the growing work. He tried on a number of occasions to explain to his corporate chiefs that he needed assistance and even drew up a comprehensive plan that would consolidate some sales territories and take the pressure off a centralized hub of distribution. But because his company was a family-owned and -managed business, which was reluctant to change and not very progressive, Carlos was in a tight spot. "I had some great ideas that would have helped me manage the entire U.S. operation in a much more efficient manner. But the old *'padrones'* who were used to a small mom-and-pop store mentality when it came to sales couldn't understand that the pressure was hurting business despite increased sales."

The old-school thinking was only part of the problem. Although Carlos spoke Spanish fluently, the company owners nevertheless had a communication problem with Carlos that can only be explained as generational differences. They couldn't understand why the young executive couldn't maintain the company clients in the "old personal style." And Carlos couldn't convince them that it just doesn't work that way with such volume and stiff competition that moves quickly.

"I needed help," Carlos said. "And I recalled that as a child my mother would often go to the local *santero* for some magickal Santeria spells whenever she was in need. The *santero* is the Santeria priest, and I always knew when my mother was on her way there because she would pack some sweet cakes and special herbs she bought at the *botanica*. I didn't know at the time that the package was an offering to one of the *orishas,* but as I learned about Santeria later in life, it all fit together. We'd go to the *santero,* he'd open the package, and within a week or so my mother was smiling again. So, I needed to smile at work once again and decided to use some Santeria magick myself."

The *orisha* Elleggua is the "keeper of the crossroads" between this world and the spirit world, so Carlos figured, what *orisha* was better to deliver a message for better communication between him and his company than the "Divine Messenger"? He was the first to admit that he didn't want to visit a *santero* out of concern that his business associates would think him into the "occult." He was especially concerned about his bosses in the Dominican Republic, who thought Santeria was a savage black magick practice. If they got wind of Carlos's supernatural bent, his job would have surely been at stake. So the desperate businessman decided to work his own spells in an effort to influence the *padrones* into accepting what he knew in his heart was a solution to their common problem.

His first step was to identify the items that would influence the *orisha* Elleggua. There are literally thousands of herbs, powders, oils, and even soaps and washes that are used in Santeria spells, so Carlos had to narrow his search. He remembered that nutmeg, when used in a special oil, was a way for Elleggua to open the avenues to opportunity. He also knew that certain candles, when mixed with herbs, would bring business prosperity. But he recalled his mother boiling pots of foul-smelling ingredients to make the candles—a task he didn't want to undertake. So Carlos acquired a ready-made candle from a *botanica* and dressed it with the proper ingredients. He reasoned that a mixture of the right elements would satisfy Elleggua regardless of the method, so he combined tradition with practicality and used his own brand of *Corporate Magick,* confident that his work problems would be settled.

Here's what Carlos used to invoke the *orisha* Elleggua and address his business communications problem with his superiors:

## Prosperity Candle

### Ingredients
  A green beeswax candle procured at a local *botanica*
  Nutmeg powder, mint leaves, violet flowers
  Nutmeg oil, coconut oil, olive oil
  Soil from the grounds around a bank

**Action**

Carlos mixed the ingredients (except the bank soil) into the olive oil until dissolved. He dressed the candle with the oil from the middle upward and lit it while invoking the *orisha* Elleggua through meditation, making for him a pathway to his superior's minds. He then sprinkled the soil around the base of the candle in a circular clockwise motion, while visualizing a productive conversation with the *padrones* of his company.

Carlos explained that although his spell was a hybrid concoction that contained ingredients of his own, it nonetheless "felt right," similar to the feeling he got as a child when his mother worked her Santeria magick, so he burned the candle for twenty-one (the number of Elleggua) consecutive evenings until it was completely gone.

"It must have been about two weeks after I burned the Santeria candle to Elleggua (I also said a prayer to St. Anthony—Elleggua's Catholic counterpart) that I began to notice a change. One of the owners' daughters who had recently graduated business school began to take an interest in the company. She called me about meeting so she could get a handle on the business, which gave me the opportunity to explain the difficult situation I was having with coordinating the sales effort in the United States. I felt I finally had a sympathetic ear in her, and my spirits began to rise. She subsequently arrived in Miami, and we spent the better part of a week going over my plans."

Carlos recounted how only a few short days after his meeting with the boss's daughter, his proposal was accepted and his sales operation in Miami materialized the way he envisioned. "The ritual renewed my faith in the *orishas*. From then on I made sure I didn't neglect my magickal Santeria roots and have since began a more intense study into the practice. You never know when you need the help of the spirits," he said.

# *Orisha* Obatala (The Father of Creation)

## *Marissa's Goal: Renew Her Abilities*

Marissa never had a problem coming up with creative new concepts for advertising campaigns while a student at New York University in Manhattan's Greenwich Village. She was especially good at creating ethnic campaigns for the Hispanic business community, considering that she was of Brazilian heritage, was bilingual, and was married to a Brazilian native. The energy just seemed to flow each time a company asked for a unique idea that would set it apart from the rest of the market. It was Marissa's forte to be able to quickly and enthusiastically deliver a campaign for her clients. Everything in her career was going well until shortly after her father passed away in early 2000. "It was just past the millennium celebration that Papa died. I felt that part of me was cut away," Marissa told me. "Little did I know that my reaction was so literal—a piece of me, my creative soul—began to disappear."

At lunch one afternoon at a café near Carmine Street, Marissa and I began to chat about her anxiety over losing her creative "juices" and how it was affecting her job. We often met to talk about spiritual matters, the occult, and especially her parents' beliefs in Santeria, and on this occasion the topic of her father's beliefs was that much more poignant. But then I asked her if she'd ever considered tapping into the mysteries of Santeria to help with her problems. I said that the *orisha* Obatala, the Father of Creation, would be the perfect spirit for her to contact for divine help. "Yes, I know about Obatala," Marissa said, and added that her father, a fine artist, often used special powders in his studio whenever he felt that he needed inspiration. So I told her that magick was staring her in her face. Her father was creative; Obatala is the "father" of creation, and her problems all centered on her blocked "creativity."

Marissa set out to use magick to get her career back on track. Together she and I mapped out how she should go about using Santeria in business. I coached her on the usefulness of the

*Corporate Magick* approach, in that any discipline will work if the magician truly believes in the outcome. In Marissa's case, the belief system was inherent; she'd been exposed to the magick of Santeria through her family. The challenge was for her to focus on the task of using nature's ingredients instead of "normal" business tools like computers and art supplies. Because she was familiar with her father's use of magickal Santeria powders, that's the path she took. Marissa was now determined to ask Obatala for guidance and assistance in getting back her creative energy. She felt confident because this particular *orisha* is the only spirit with both male and female sides.

Marissa knew enough about her religion to realize that an offering, or an *ebo,* must be provided to the spirit out of respect, which could include either "addimui" (candles, flowers, or fruits) or a personal request like wearing certain items or giving up a bad habit. She chose to create an amulet that she could use and take with her to her agency undetected. A white pouch with red and purple stripes (Obatala's affiliated colors) was Marissa's choice. She filled it with a special blend of seven powdered herbs and treated it with gardenia oil, a favorite of Obatala's, which is legendary for bringing clarity to the mind of the user.

## Magickal Pouch Amulet

### Ingredients
Herbs for Obatala: clove; dragon's blood; frankincense; pine; orris; lavender; mugwort; gardenia oil. Pouch: White satin pouch with red and purple adornments.

### Action
Marissa's ceremony began with the banging of the tall ceremonial drums that had been passed down through her family. The rhythmic pounding was her way of entering a meditative state and the traditional beginning for most Santeria ceremonies and rituals. The mesmerizing beat of the *orisha,* called an *oru* in Santeria, had a dual effect on Marissa. She had forgotten how relaxing and primal the sounds were, helping her enjoy a respite

from the worry over not being at her creative best. But the drums also allowed her mind to focus on the task at hand— preparing the mixture of herbs for the powder she was offering to Obatala. The magickal powder was the main ingredient in Marissa's magickal pouch and the catalyst that would eventually get her back in her creative groove, so she painstakingly measured each herb by hand, intuitively adding the amounts. As she mixed the materials, she felt at once that she was gaining her mental strength once again. She caressed the bag with the gardenia oil and literally felt the pouch come alive. In typical Santeria fashion, she threw herself on the floor of her apartment facedown, hands outstretched to her sides, to invoke the spirit of Obatala. "I knew Obatala's presence was near. I felt my amulet pulse with his power, and before long I knew I would be back on top," she said.

For the next month Marissa carried her magickal pouch whenever a business meeting called. One evening over dinner with friends, she had an idea for a slogan and character for a company she happened to see advertised on a billboard on her way to the restaurant. With renewed confidence and excitement over her idea, she called the company the next morning and, in a week's time, landed the account.

## *Orisha* Chango (God of Power)

### *Anthony's Goal: Prevent a Hostile Takeover*

Anthony and his partner in his franchised dry-cleaning business had not been getting along for nearly a year. Each time Anthony, a progressive thinker and a technology maven, suggested a new procedure to incorporate technical advances into the company's chain of thirty-five stores, his partner, Alan, resisted. In most cases, Anthony said that Alan was simply being stubborn, trying everything in his power to get Anthony disgusted with the business so he would eventually sell his portion to Alan. But the business was Anthony's original idea and was very successful. The standoff became a matter of economic sense and pride, and Anthony did not want to relent.

But the situation flared up into a hostile takeover scenario when Alan, the owner of another company, decided to buy as much as he could of the dry-cleaning company's stock from the store shareholders in an effort to gain control. "Alan was willing to pay the shareholders double and triple what the stock was worth and guarantee them their jobs if they'd sell to him," Anthony said. "He would have a controlling number of shares if most of the store managers sold, so I was in a bind."

Fortunately for Anthony, help was just around the corner— literally. A Latina woman named Carla, who opened a small *botanica* near Anthony's establishment, quickly became the small businessman's friend and confidante. They often spent hours discussing the occult arts and how magick can work in everyday life. Anthony became fascinated by Carla's stories of how magick— particularly the workings of Santeria—had helped many of her friends in their business and personal lives through the use of natural ingredients and true belief. In fact, Carla had given Anthony a magickal "tree stick," commonly used in a sect of Santeria, called *palo monte*. The *palo jeringa* stick Carla gave Anthony was to help him in his strained love life at the time. He remembered her mentioning that the tree stick was empowered by a god named Chango, whom she said was very powerful—in fact, he was the god of power and could work incredibly strong magick in most any dire circumstance.

The hostile takeover qualified as "dire" in Anthony's mind. He immediately sought Carla's help and the power of Santeria, particularly the *orisha* Chango's assistance. And Carla was prepared to meet the challenge. She told Anthony that he needed magick that normally would require animal sacrifice, but she understood his concerns so she suggested that Anthony prepare a special oil lamp, called the "Victory Lamp," from a book she gave him for the *orisha* Chango to ensure that his business would be saved. Oil lamps, Carla explained, are used primarily for blessings and special requests, and in Anthony's case, he needed both.

Anthony admitted to me that he was reluctant at first to resort to calling on Santeria spirits for help in winning his business battles, but he assured me that he'd tried every other method without much success and his back was against the wall. "People I told thought I was crazy, but I thought, hey, it's no more crazy than people praying in church, lighting candles, and taping money to the bottom of saints' statues. And I felt at ease with Carla; she had a peaceful presence, yet I sensed she had some deep hidden knowledge. And on top of it all, the *palo* tree stick she gave me got me and my girlfriend back together."

## Chango's Victory Oil Lamp *

**Ingredients**

   Large ceramic bowl
   Powdered *palo vence batalla* (from *botanica*)
   Pomegranate juice
   Clove powder
   Sliced plantano
   Sliced red apples
   1 tablespoon red precipitate powder
   2 cups olive oil
   Cinnamon powder
   Honey
   Red wine
   Six pennies
   Floating night-light

**Action**

Carla instructed Anthony to follow the instruction in the book and write his name six times on a piece of paper, place it at the bottom of the bowl, and place the six pennies on top. He was to then add the pomegranate juice and place six plantanos and six pieces of red apple each separately into the mixture. While doing this, Anthony was to picture the spirit Chango intervening in any confrontation he was having with his partner, Alan. It was diffi-

---

*Source *Santeria: Candles, Herbs, Incense, Oils* by Carlos Montengro.

cult for Anthony at first because he had no magickal training, but his faith in Carla kept him focused. Once the picture was clear in Anthony's mind, he added the rest of the ingredients into the ceramic bowl and floated the night-light for six consecutive days. On the seventh day, Anthony was to write Alan's name on a piece of red cloth, wrap the lamp in it, and place it in the woods. He made the trip to the closest wooded area and placed the lamp next to a tree that ironically had the word "Chuck" carved into it. Not "Chango," but close enough for this new magician. The next step was for Anthony to await the power that would bring him victory over his nemesis and overcome his business obstacles.

Days later, he visited Carla at her *botanica* and explained that he'd followed the book's instructions but nothing had happened. Alan was gaining momentum and Anthony felt helpless. Carla explained that the lamp's magick would not work if Anthony faltered in his will to make it work. She assured him that the "power" would be delivered to him. And it was.

Alan suddenly withdrew his bid to take over the company and informed Anthony that he actually wanted to sell *his* share. Anthony was stunned, but it wasn't until a week later that he found out that Alan had been audited by the IRS and was in deep financial trouble.

## *Orisha* Oggun (The God of Labor)

### *Philip's Goal: Fire a Disruptive Employee*

It's usually a fairly simple process: A person's not doing his job or is causing a problem, so he must be let go. Not so in the world of civil service. And Philip, a supervisor in a social services office in New Orleans, discovered this reality the hard way when a young woman defied all of the duties of her job and office. She was constantly late, abusive to clients, a gossip, and often disrespected her superiors. But because the termination process for civil servants is a difficult one to say the least, Philip needed help from the *orishas*.

In New Orleans, Philip explained, using the occult is not thought of as weird or offbeat as in other parts of the country. And considering that Philip's neighborhood was a center for Afro-Caribbean beliefs, he had no problem getting some supernatural help.

It became a simple matter of going to the local *botanica* and asking the *babalawo* (high priest) of the local Santeria sect to divine the answer to his problem. The *babalawo* used the customary seashells and told Philip that what he needed was to ask the *orisha* Oggun, the master of workers, to eliminate this person—but Philip would have to perform a simple "dirt spell." Philip explained to me that soil is a very powerful element in Santeria because it is literally the "mother earth" and a natural substance that has been around for eons. Dirt from roads, especially crossroads, is considered extremely powerful.

## Dirt Spell to Eliminate Someone

### Ingredients
Soil from the bottom of the shoe of the person you want gone. Dirt from four cemeteries. A sheet of the personal stationery of the person or a sheet of paper he has handled. A metal tray.

### Action
Mix soil with the dirt from four cemeteries. Write the person's name on the paper. Sprinkle the dirt over the paper and place it on the metal tray. The *babalawo* told Philip at his divination that he must make the mixture of dirt and for seven days light a black candle and recite his wishes to Oggun seven times. On the eighth day, Philip was to sprinkle the dirt mixture on the desk or seat of the person who was disrupting his career and his coworkers' peace of mind. "You may wonder why I just didn't flat-out fire this person," Philip said. "But unless there's some serious reason—and I mean violent threats or bizarre actions—terminating

a civil servant is next to impossible." So, determined to end his problem, Philip managed to scrape some dirt off the running shoes that the employee kept under her desk. He then gathered the other ingredients and recited his call to Oggun for seven consecutive days.

With his magickal soil in hand on a Monday morning exactly eight days after working his Santeria spell, Philip sprinkled the dirt on the seat of his malcontent subordinate. "I did everything the priest told me to do. I even traveled for miles to find cemetery dirt, but nothing happened to my employee to make her leave the job. Until two months later . . ." Philip explained that his troubles were over when he discovered his problem employee was getting married and moving to Texas. And typical of her inconsiderate nature, but joyfully accepted nonetheless, she gave only a week's notice.

# *Orisha* Oshun (Goddess of Money)

## *Denise's Goal: Get Financing for Her Beauty Salon*

After exhausting every known source of business capital, including friends, relatives, banks, credit card companies, and savings accounts, to acquire the hundred thousand dollars she needed to keep her fledgling beauty salon business afloat, Denise was ready to call it quits. Although her business in the Crown Heights section of Brooklyn, New York, was well accepted by the local clientele and the bills were being met, Denise needed the extra money to pay for more modern equipment and another person to help out. If she couldn't get her business in better shape soon, she would lose customers to a new chain that was entering the neighborhood. To add to her woes, she was already overextended in personal and business debt, so she was not a desirable candidate for any lender.

Her luck began to change one evening when Mrs. Bolivar came in for her regular appointment. The middle-aged woman often spoke to Denise about the wonder of Santeria that she experienced as a child in Cuba. She recounted the many humid nights of sacrifices and ritual dances with men and women writhing on the dirt floors in celebration of the *orishas*. Denise was often disturbed about the animal sacrifices, but when Mrs. Bolivar explained that the practice was as old as most formal religions in her country and that the animals did not suffer, Denise ignored her minor repulsion because she was enthralled by the woman's mesmerizing tales of how magick was conjured and ultimately worked. Mrs. Bolivar would recount stories of the dreaded *nganga*—a cauldron filled with human remains and insects that was the favorite tool of the *mayombero,* the black magick priests. She'd also tell of the *orishas,* on the other hand, whose role as the benefactors of humans played a major part in the lives of those who practiced Santeria.

When the conversation at hand turned to Denise's money woes, Mrs. Bolivar stated matter-of-factly: "Just do a money spell to Oshun, darlin', and the loan will be yours." Needless to say, Denise was taken aback and asked Mrs. Bolivar how a simple spell could get her a hundred thousand dollars. Denise was no stranger to the world of Afro-Caribbean beliefs, having heard many stories from her family members over the years, but when it came to cold hard cash, she was skeptical. The wise woman simply smiled and said that Denise had to believe as hard as she could possibly believe that Oshun would come to her aid—and she would. "She's the goddess of money, baby. She will help you. Go do the spell and before you do, clean your mind of everything and picture a beautiful peacock flying toward heaven. Then you will be in touch with Oshun."

When Denise asked me if she thought it was "safe" to work the magick because she thought Mrs. Bolivar's instructions about the "peacock" seemed odd, I mentioned to her that the peacock is often a symbolic association of the Oshun mythos and that if she felt she needed the help, she should go for it. I explained that there are many corporate magicians in the world, and we'd welcome her to our ranks. I recommended two spells. The next step was Denise's.

## Two Spells for Obtaining Money

1. The magician must go to a bank where the loan is desired, get change of a dollar from one of the tellers, write the name of the bank on a piece of paper, and place five of the coins on top of the paper. Place five mint leaves on top of the coins and fill a saucer with *aceite intraquilo* and a bit of quicksilver. Float the wick and cork of a night-light in the oil and light for one hour every day at noon for five days.*
2. Put 2 cups of cosmetic alcohol S.D. (40 proof) in a glass bottle.
   Add:
   - 25 drops cinnamon tincture
   - 15 drops *abre camino* herb tincture
   - 15 drops *boton de oro* tincture
   - 10 drops nutmeg tincture
   Seal in the bottle for seven days before use.†

**Action**

Denise followed the instructions and made her perfume, finding everything she needed from a *botanica* on the Upper West Side of Manhattan. She reasoned that wearing the perfume while going to the bank would be a one–two magickal punch, and she needed all the help she could get. The next morning, she went to a local bank and submitted her loan application while keeping the perfume's hidden power in mind, wondering if it was permeating and charging the air around her.

The required five days passed, and the night before she ventured to the bank Denise "cleansed her mind," as Mrs. Bolivar requested, visualizing a beautifully colored peacock, symbolic of Oshun, soaring into the blue heavens. In what she described as a "half-dream state," somewhere between sleep and wakefulness, Denise heard the voice of Oshun speaking to her in a calming manner, saying that she would receive what she needed, but not

---

*Spell from *Santeria: African Magick in Latin America* by Migene Gonzales-Wippler.
†Spell from *Santeria: Candles, Herbs, Incense, Oils* by Carlos Montengro.

in the way she expected. Although she was amazed at the vividness of the experience and that she truly believed she contacted the *orisha,* she was a bit disappointed that the message was so vague. "I had faith that the magick would work. Funny . . . I was a little skeptical before I started the ritual, but once I was into it my perspective changed," she said. I told Denise that this is a common occurrence for novice magicians. The process of *performing* the magick is actually a catalyst for belief.

After a week's time, Denise was shocked to learn her loan had not been approved. She was now faced with an eleventh-hour decision to close the business. She left the shop that evening, disappointed that the magick hadn't worked and went home. She listened to the messages on her answering machine—one of which quickly saddened her but quickly turned out to be a blessing. Her great-aunt had passed away, and she was the sole heir of an estate that included a house worth in excess of $200,000. At the reading of the will, Denise was stunned to see her great-aunt's favorite vase filled with a flowing, colorful, three-foot-high bunch of *peacock* feathers.

## *Orisha* Orunla (God of Prophecy)

### *Sam's Goal: Win in the Stock Market*

Sam's goal was simple: Buy stocks that would rise in value over the long term so he could provide a good college education and nest egg for his children. He had fifty thousand dollars to play with, didn't trust brokers, and had been burned by a bad tip from his brother-in-law in the early 1990s. So when he saw a psychic at a local fair giving someone stock advice and then watched that person drive away in a Mercedes convertible, he thought there must be something to divining the future.

Sam's wife, Elaine, told him of her cousin Matilda, who practiced Santeria and who was often right on the money when it came to foretelling the future. Sam remembered visiting Matilda and being amazed at the number of statues of saints in her living room; she'd told him that all answers originate from the "Table of Ifa," the Santeria altar of divination. He also remembered that she'd never had a full-time job yet seemed to live more comfortably than him. "I asked how she operated, and my wife said she communicated with the spirit called Orunla, who foretold the future. I asked if she would do it for me, and we visited her the next day," Sam recalled.

## Candle Spell to Orunla

### Ingredients
Yellow and green candles
Frankincense incense
Acacia oil
Jasmine oil
(Dress the green candle with acacia oil and dress the yellow candle with jasmine oil.)
One-dollar bill
Cinnamon, anisette, or coconut sweet roll

### Action
Because Sam was an absolute beginner in the world of magick, his wife Elaine, with the help of Matilda, coached the investor on how to prepare his will to tap into the energy of the universe and summon Orunla to divine some winning stocks. Sam's focus of concentration was on a few major stock offerings, so Matilda advised that he get a copy of the *Wall Street Journal*, find the stock symbols he was interested in, write them down on the outer horizontal edges of the dollar bill, and place the bill flat on a table tightly between the candles.

Sam was then told to concentrate on seeing his chosen stock prices rise incredibly high and fast and him jumping with joy. Then he was to give thanks to Orunla by offering a cinnamon, anisette, or coconut sweet roll. Next, he was to light the candles and observe to see which symbol was first touched by the dripping wax. That was to be his stock of choice.

The following day Sam bought one hundred shares of the

stock indicated by the melting wax. In three months the stock split, and Sam saw a healthy profit. He then began a weekly ritual to Orunla and has been choosing stocks through spiritual influence ever since.

## *Orisha* Yemaya (Goddess of Protection)

### *Ray's Goal: Stop a Corporate Backstabber*

We've all faced this scenario in our business careers: Someone is either jealous of our abilities or is seeking to push us out of our position for his own sake. And it happened to Ray much too soon after he was promoted to senior vice president of sales at a major health care company in Palm Beach, Florida. The onslaught was fast and furious, as Ray's nemesis slung all manner of gossip and badmouth tactics at anyone who would listen to his diabolical ramblings. Ray tried to ignore the situation and chalk it up to just another insecure, jealous coworker, but when Ray was called into the chairman's office to explain why he had "deliberately reported bad sales figures"—according to the rabble-rouser—Ray had had enough.

What the troublemaker didn't bargain for was that Ray was an astute practitioner of both voodoo and Santeria, and although he only resorted to the use of magick for positive purposes, he had to defend himself against a person who was threatening his livelihood. Even under these dire circumstances, Ray knew that he could use good magick to deflect the evil in his office. He had at his disposal much more malevolent spells, curses, and charms that he could attack with, but instead Ray chose to call on the *orisha* Yemaya, the mother of the seven seas and the great protector. His reasoning was that magick power of great ferocity would just be wasted on such a pathetically insecure individual.

Ray decided to make a black rag doll, a Santeria protection fetish, infused with elements of sympathetic magick with Yemaya and personal effects of his rival. The black doll sits in close proximity to the person it's defending and, if touched by the offender, releases serious magickal retribution in the form of physical and mental discomfort.

## The Black Doll

**Ingredients**
  Heavy black cloth
  White bone buttons
  String to bead a necklace
  White and blue beads
  Basil, mugwort, camphor herbs
  Small pouch

**Action**
With drum music beating in the background, Ray took up scissors and began cutting the crude pattern of a human figure out of a swath of black cloth. The black doll figure, about twelve inches high, was carefully sewn together but left open at the neck so it could be filled with cotton stuffing. As Ray constructed his fetish, he pictured his business foe slowly disappearing from the office environment and apologizing to all concerned about his lying and political machinations. As the drums pounded louder, Ray worked himself into a frenzy of creation, finishing the doll in a matter of minutes. He then attached the bone eyes to the face and asked for Yemaya to bless it and empower it with her magickal fire.

   Once Ray completed stringing the white and blue (colors of Yemaya) beads, he placed the string around the doll's neck. He filled a pouch with basil, mugwort, and camphor and pinned it to the doll. Ray then conducted a complete ritual dedicated to Yemaya. He described it like this: "I can only tell you that this was one of the most intense rituals and offerings I ever conducted. I used magick for business before, but I never needed the help so desperately as in this circumstance. I pulled out all of the stops and even considered using a blood sacrifice, but I used dragon's blood instead."

   The doll was placed on a file cabinet near Ray's desk, hidden so as not to attract attention, but that wasn't important. Just being in the office started the magick to work. "He didn't stop with the backstabbing, but something curious began to occur," Ray said. "He was concentrating so much on making me look bad that he was making mistakes himself and not realizing them. Small ones at first, but then they became larger and larger until it came to a head one day in the boss's office." When he was cornered about his ineptitude, the company rat fabricated a ridiculously lame story about Ray stealing his toothbrush from the men's room. When the boss heard such a petty excuse, he had no recourse but to let the man go—on the spot. And, by the way, Ray *did* take the offender's toothbrush, and he placed the bristles in the black doll's pouch—just for insurance!

## INSTANT MAGICK INDEX CARD

### Santeria Spell for General Business Prosperity

Seven African Powers candle from a *botanica*
Bottle of dragon's blood oil
Elleggua candle dressing oil
Flat white dish

Dress the candle with the Elleggua oil. Pour 20 drops of dragon's blood on a white dish. Concentrate on the dragon's blood oil and send your wishes to the *orisha* Elleggua.
Do this for seven consecutive days. On the seventh day ask the *Corporate Magick* Cabal for the same assistance.

CHAPTER **8**

# The Kabbalah—Become a Master of the Universe

O f all of the magickal and esoteric mystery schools ever known, the arcane discipline known as the Kabbalah is by far the most intricate, involved, confusing, and daunting. Arcane lore maintains that by studying the Kabbalah, man can communicate with the divine, summon the angels to do his bidding, and truly know his very soul. That being said, the Kabbalah can be a powerful ally in the business world. And by mastering some basic principles, the corporate magician will hone meditative skills that will assist in every kind of magick, from simple ceremony to astral travel, right into your company's boardroom.

Proponents will tell you that the painstakingly complex methods and requirements for studying and using the Kabbalah are justified because the "true believers" know that the mystical system is a blueprint for man to regain his "fall from grace." It is said that the ancient study was either taught to the angels by God himself, and then given to Adam, or handed down to Moses during the "burning bush" episode, and then passed down by word of mouth to the generations of prophets outlined in the Bible. Much of the lofty thinking of the Kabbalah stems from the fact that although there is a practical magickal use for the Kabbalah, the system centers on creation, the soul, divinity, and how humans can actually communicate with God. Although essentially a Judaic religious/mystical art steeped in religious Hebrew law over the centuries, the Kabbalah has actually become a mixture of Eastern and Western occult schools, evolving into the most "intellectualized" magick system in the occult world.

Whichever path you take—strict adherence to Judaic interpretation or the more blended practice often referred to as "Hermetic" Kabbalah—most occultists agree that the path was constructed by divine intervention, and it's an inherently powerful system held to be a direct pathway to knowing the mysteries of life—even the universe itself. Pretty lofty stuff, even for the mystically inclined.

So you're probably asking: If it's so confusing, how will it be used in business, and why do we need to know its history? Well, the basis of anything that helps the subconscious mind better absorb principles is beneficial, and as you'll soon discover, using the subconscious along with the conscious mind is a cornerstone of using the Kabbalah. A little history will benefit you later on. You many not know macroeconomic theories, but it helps to know that it's the basis of how we live with money.

The Kabbalah is said to have originated as far back as the first century. Many of its students maintain that the magickal power derived from the system comes from the unwritten "oral" law straight from God and given to Moses the same time he received the written law. According to Jewish tradition, the Torah, the first five books of the Old Testament, contain the written law that maps out God's plans for creation. By studying the Torah, it is believed that you can unlock all mysteries. So, the bottom line is that God dictated a holy manual but also communicated some whispered secrets to prophets, which together provide humanity with the Kabbalah—a system that allows users to be "Masters of Mystery," "Masters of Knowledge," and "Those Who Know."

The word "Kabbalah," literally translates to the phrase "to receive." What mystics and magicians receive from studying this discipline is secret knowledge about a number of life mysteries, including angels, numerology, functions of the body, dreams, the tarot, astrology, meditation, and how to manipulate all of these things with the help of divine intervention. Students can become heavily involved and study numerous books about just one piece of the Kabbalah puzzle—say, *gematria*, the use of numbers and how they translate with Hebrew letters. For *Corporate Magick* purposes we will concentrate only on the more practical methods of achieving worldly benefits as opposed to spiritual elevation.

The "non-Jewish," or Hermetic form of the magick has been influenced by a number of magickal luminaries, including the magicians of the Golden Dawn and the Freemasons, and has also been linked to the work of the Corpus Hermiticum of legendary mage Hermes Trismegistus, which melds Christianity and Egyptian mysticism centering on the god Thoth. This hybrid type of Kabbalah is also referred to as the "Western Mystery Tradition."

Of course we'd all love to understand the workings of the universe and have the thousands of hours available to us to complete the deep study of the Kabbalah. And it would be wonderful to magickally open the many astounding doors to the universe, but we're most concerned with how the Kabbalah can help us be successful, and that's where *Corporate Magick* kicks in. I have taken the key elements of the Kabbalah—the Tree of Life and its map of "Sephiroth," or spherical icons, often called the "Splendid Lights" (see figure 3)—and devised a method of using them so that we're able to organize the energies of the Kabbalah in a way that makes sense to our practical Western minds.

Using the Tree of Life allows us to channel the energies of the Kabbalah through an intricate diagram that maps out how man and the divine are related by virtue of how they're represented in the same universe. The body of God (called Adam Kadmon) is the whole of the entire universe, and the body of man is the microcosm that holds a universe of its own. Before I start waxing philosophical here—after all, what we're interested in is managing our finances, never mind the cosmos—let's just say that by understanding what the Tree of Life represents, you'll be better able to use its parts in creating your own magick.

What makes the Kabbalah such an interesting and pragmatic tool to include in the *Corporate Magick* system is that it simply works, and thousands of magicians have proven that it works.

## FIG. 3 The Spheres and Their Effect on Business

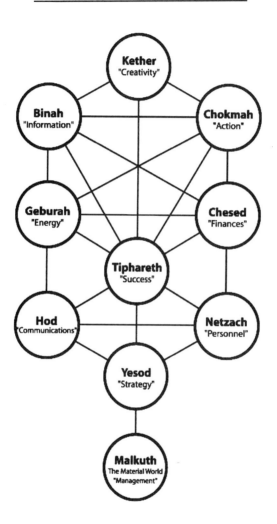

The Kabbalah also requires that the magician meditate—a powerful tool that will assist you in any occult study. The practical advantages of using the Kabbalah are twofold: First, a major part of its modus operandi is ceremony and ritual that can be conducted

by following some simple steps. By grasping the basic construc-
tion of the Kabbalah's Tree of Life and all its "correspondences,"
the system can be manipulated and customized to serve the magician in almost any endeavor. The second aspect of the
Kabbalah that makes it a natural for business magicians is that it
has a solid base in the practical material world as well as in the
spiritual, so it provides the magician with a path to using the
magick effectively. And despite its complicated structure, the Tree
of Life map and its influences can be adapted to each individual's
goal if the magician remains focused on what he wants. Although
most students of the Kabbalah get caught up in its deep, dark secrets revealing universal truths, you'll learn that there are in fact
a number of portions of the Kabbalah strictly designed to unlock
the mysteries that help in *this* world.

As I've already pointed out, the Kabbalah can be foreboding
even to the highest magickal adept. We're starting simple in *Corporate Magick* and will begin with understanding the Kabbalah's
Sephiroth—the spheres of influence on the Tree of Life map—
and how they are affected by their "correspondences": elements,
colors, gems, nature, angels, names, and so forth. We'll work closely
with the sphere "Malkuth," the lowest level of consciousness on
the map, which represents the creation of our world and serves as
the center of the material desires. I am going to cut through the
thousands of hours of required study and get to the heart of what
makes the Kabbalah such a powerful magickal tool, and what
that is in a nutshell is the will of the magician, just as it is with any
occult discipline. We'll harness the energies of the Kabbalah and
use them for our workaday wishes.

Despite criticism that may be launched by magickal and religious experts alike, who may be dismayed that the purity of the
Kabbalah is being somehow cheapened and manipulated to its
lowest form, even hard-core traditionalists will admit that the
Kabbalah is most effective when the Tree of Life is worked upon
for material gain where the magician becomes the living conduit
drawing down the power (lightning) from the universe itself.
This is in fact the ultimate goal of working the Kabbalah—to en-
lighten and infuse the magician with power. So to say that using

it just for pleasure and comfort is blasphemous is solely a matter of opinion. Where *Corporate Magick* is concerned, the primary reason magick exists is to aid the magician. There wouldn't be divine influence in the Kabbalah if it weren't intended to aid humanity. As long as it harms none, so be it.

Furthermore, the Kabbalah is also sometimes compared to yoga, and in fact, is often referred to as the "yoga of the Western world." An analogy can be drawn to yoga in that you don't have to know all the many, many mystic philosophies, *pranas*, mantras, *asanas*, and so on to reap the benefits of the system. And because of the incredible number of intricacies involved with the system, most magicians don't even agree on a number of the methods used, much less whether they are orthodox or not. There are also those who claim that it's downright dangerous to use the Kabbalah ceremonies if you are not absolutely certain of how to manipulate the Tree and its power. They claim that, because different paths on the Tree represent positive and negative energy flows, if a magician performs a ceremony that directs the wrong flow, the results can be disastrous. There is some truth to this: All magickal bodies are tools, and like any tool, if the Kabbalah is not handled properly, bad things can happen. It is true that the Tree of Life needs to be in balance with its energies in order to work. But to say that there's "danger" is a bit dramatic unless you are intentionally summoning demons or are at such an advanced stage as a magician that you are using elementals (spirits) to do your bidding. If you follow the *Corporate Magick* approach that maps out positive, tested, and balanced paths, then your magick will be safe and effective.

---

## CASE STUDY
## ROBIN'S TREE OF "*LIFE*-LIHOOD"

---

Robin, a young woman who's been fascinated with angels since she was a young child, became naturally attracted to the Kabbalah some years ago when she learned that the system often calls on the archangels for help through the use of the divine names—a correspondence of the system. She was determined to advance her career and be recognized for the hard work she was doing in order to earn a promotion she felt was long overdue. Although not an expert in using the system, Robin had the Tree of Life glyph in a poster on her bedroom wall and over the years memorized each Sephira sphere and its major representation. Knowing that it was the "glory" of a job well done she was after, and remembering that the sphere Hod represented glory on the Tree, Robin made it her business to work a little magickal business of her own.

"I always knew that the Kabbalah and the Tree of Life had special meaning to me because of the archangels, Michael, Gabriel, Raphael, and Uriel," Robin said. "I also knew that I had to build a representative Tree of Life that mimicked my life so I could then manipulate the Sephiroth and call on the angels for help." What's more, Robin knew of a Kabbalah ritual targeted at the archangel Michael—her favorite—but it could only be performed on her birthday. "I read in a book about the Kabbalah that if I soaked a red strip of cloth in salt water, placed it over my eyes, and mailed it to 'Michael Arch' at the exact opposite longitude and latitude of where I was born, my wishes would be answered,"* Robin said.

She followed the instructions to the letter, mailing the strip on her birthday to the fictitious name on the opposite point on the globe. The letter contained her real return address because, according to the book's author, the letter, although almost foolproof, must be returned to the magician before the magick can take effect.

But Robin didn't sit back and wait for the mystical returned posting. Her faith in the Kabbalah, coupled with the fact that she was a seasoned business pro, made her realize that she needed to take extra measures to assure that her magick would work. Besides sending the magickal letter to Michael, Robin also constructed her own Tree of Life map out of items she took from her office—an easy task because she was working in a New York advertising agency at the time. The new magician reasoned, and rightly so, that by using items from her job—the environment she wanted to influence—the sympathetic magick would act as an extra advantage in her Kabbalah workings. She gathered a large two- by three-foot art board, color markers, and strips of an orange metallic paper. Her investigation into the workings of the

*From *A Kabbalah for the Modern World* by Migene Gonzales-Wippler.

Kabbalah revealed that the color orange—the color of the Sephira Hod that deals directly with business matters—would work well as "divine" elements on her Tree.

The key methods of using the Tree of Life to work at the material level is to identify the sphere—the Sephira—that will "touch" your subconscious level and open the doors to fulfilling your wishes. Each Sephira has elements and correspondences that address particular areas of concern. And because Robin also called on the archangel Michael for help, she had to use the right combinations of Sephira and calling of the holy name of the angels.

"I constructed a ritual on my Tree [a benefit of the Kabbalah Tree is that it can be "customized" to the individual and continue to be powerful in multiple manifestations] with the sephira of Hod. This is the level of consciousness that deals directly with business matters and 'glory.' I had plenty of guts, but rarely received the glory. So Hod and its relation to business matters was a natural. Hod's corresponding angel is Michael, my assisting angel of choice, the Great Protector, whom I already invoked through the red cloth ritual. I vibrated the name of Michael by saying his name over and over, each time increasing the intensity of my enunciation. My purpose was to flow the Kabbalah energy to Michael through Hod," Robin explained.

Robin proceeded to meditate on her Sephira in an attempt to reach the Kabbalah's plane of consciousness where she could find out how to get her superiors to value her worth. Because she was an old pro at meditation, it didn't take her long to feel the Sephira Hod open its doors to her. "It was like a warm globe undulating and beckoning me into its core. I realized I was sitting on my bed at home, but somehow my thoughts and brain were focused on this beautiful sphere. I guess that's why they call them the 'Splendid Lights.' I couldn't take my eyes off of its brilliance. I immediately realized that I was entering a place of great cosmic age and reverence and I knew I would receive the answers I was seeking."

What happened next was what Robin described as "divine intervention." She recounted how her archangel guide, Michael, appeared to her not in flowing white robes with wings, but as a young, well-dressed man, similar to the men she deals with in business every day. Needless to say, she was stunned to see a being of any kind while in this meditative state, but she felt totally comfortable and happy to be in his presence. Michael took Robin by the hand and led her to a series of doors. He told her that behind one of the doors she would discover the secret that would energize her career.

Suddenly vaulted out of her meditation, Robin found herself lying on her bed, totally relaxed but with a vivid memory of what had just occurred. It was a puzzle of sorts—knowing that the secret was behind a door—but she was impatient to get to the bottom of the message from the Kabbalah's realm. What happened next can only be explained by first understanding something called the Path of the Flaming Sword, or the energy lightning that is said to have been the divine swath cut through the creation of the universe represented in the Tree of Life. The next day at work, Robin decided to clean out her office closet, which was long overdue. While reaching for a box on the top shelf, she was unexpectedly knocked back into her chair by a power that surged through her body. At first she thought she had touched a loose electrical wire, but then realized nothing was exposed. As she sat in her chair, she gazed toward the top of the shelf and saw a file marked "Cleos," which contained hundreds of award-winning print ads someone had collected over the years. That's when it dawned on her!

"I looked at the old ads and realized they would be the perfect background material for one of our major clients who wanted a nostalgic campaign concept. I had seen the folder many times but it never occurred to me to use old stuff for a new campaign," Robin said. Well the rest fell into place. Robin suggested the old ads as a basis for the client's campaign and her superiors were thrilled. "Using the old file just never registered before Michael 'opened the door' for me," Robin quipped. And by the way, Robin received her returned letter to Michael Arch on the exact day she received her new promotion.

---

# Working the Kabbalah

Okay, so you're sold on the idea that the Kabbalah can make you a "Master of the Universe," or at the very least open your subconscious mind to the many mysteries and, more importantly, the tools to help you gain material success in the real world.

What you've read so far about the Kabbalah, even though it may sound confusing at times, has only scratched the surface. There are many, many approaches, methods, and Kabbalah connections to different occult systems, including astrology, the tarot, numerology, cryptology, and more, which work together and can be employed in our magickal workings. And I encourage you to continue your study more deeply into this fascinating school if you're so inclined, because the resulting wonders far transcend just the business benefits we're seeking here. One of the more simplistic explanations of the Kabbalah says that God emanated his force through the universe creating the Sephiroth, and man's soul began its journey from heavenly being to earthbound mortal down through the spheres. With the help of the Kabbalah, the soul can find its way back to God. So you see, although *Corporate Magick* is useful and we've just employed a piece of the Kabbalah for our immediate tasks, the system can open numerous secret doors.

There are many excellent books and essays that can be found on the Internet and in bookstores, some of which are listed in the Appendix: Resources section in the back of this book.

That being said, let's get down to the results-oriented method *Corporate Magick* provides for getting what you need by using the Kabbalah. The bottom line is this: The Kabbalah is a great magickal source for solving almost any business problem, and *you will get answers to all of your business questions!* Follow the steps outlined below and the doors of the Kabbalah will be opened to you.

1. **Choose a sphere.** Choose a Sephira sphere of influence on the Tree of Life map (see figure 3) that represents the results (the correspondences) you are attempting to achieve.

2. **Prepare.** Meditate to clear your mind and help it focus; alter your state of consciousness.

3. **Identify your assistant.** Identify the astral beings—angels and gods—you will call upon for aid.

4. **Work the energy.** Resonate the energies through verbal recitation; feel the lightning surge, touch the power.

5. **Ask for help.** Discuss your wishes on the astral plane.

6. **Act on the magick.** Work your magick immediately by putting the results into action.

7. **Create your master self.** Cultivate your new "Master" magickal body.

# Choose a Sphere

This is your first step in using the Kabbalah as a practical tool. Think of it as choosing internal documents of a company you want to invest in, or perhaps having lunch with the CEO of a firm you've been dying to work for. The information is right there at hand; all you need to do is absorb it and make some decisions based on the facts presented. Your choice is crucial to the outcome you desire, so choose the Sephiroth that will allow you entrance into the temples of the Kabbalah where the angels and gods you seek are available. Refer to the chart on page 137, which lists each of the ten Sephiroth and the business attributes with which they correspond. Keep in mind that on the Tree of Life, the lower the sphere is on the tree, the more involved with the material world it will be. As you can see, Malkuth is probably the sphere that will most benefit the corporate magician, but the beauty of the Kabbalah is that it is customizable and can work at any stage.

And remember, your sphere will be influenced by one of the Tree's three pillars: The left pillar has a negative/female/passive influence; the right pillar has a positive/male/active influence; and the center pillar is neutral and balanced, acting as a mediator to establish equilibrium. So consider the effect the pillar will have on your sphere of choice. For example, imagine you choose to use the sphere Geburah to gain information on your enemies. This sphere is on the passive pillar, so the information you will receive will have to be ascertained in a clever, covert method instead of as a full-blown demand.

Some occultists claim that the magician cannot work one side of the Tree of Life without also working in pairs with its counterpart on the opposite pillar because the spheres' counterparts create balance in the universe, and to upset this balance will prohibit the magick. There is also a method of massaging the Kabbalah that groups the Sephiroth into "triads"—a series of triangles that point to areas of the Tree of Life. The use of the triads is primarily for attaining higher spiritual standing and as such can be studied by those furthering their Kabbalastic curiosity. But because our focus is tuned to practical business matters, not to seeking answers to the mysteries of the universe, our methods will not be affected by these "higher" pursuits.

Choose your sphere based on the combination of its literal meaning and its business attribute. If you are seeking knowledge, choose Binah. Then check its pillar, which is passive. Then use its color—black—as an element in your ritual. You can then call on its corresponding angel or god name to assist you. Keep in mind that the *Corporate Magick* Cabal is also available twenty-four hours a day, and can be summoned during your meditation phase to assist you before or during your working. The Cabal can assist with your angel or deity or can be your single source of help. Just communicate with the Cabal once you've entered the gateway of your sphere and converse with the Cabal as you would with your chosen angel or deity.

## The Sephiroth and Their Business Effects

| Name | Meaning | Business | Color | Angel/God |
|------|---------|----------|-------|-----------|
| Kether | Crown | Creativity | White | Metatron/Creator |
| Chokmah | Wisdom | Action | Gray | Ratzkiel/Father |
| Binah | Knowledge | Information | Black | Tzafkiel/Mother |
| Chesed | Mercy | Finances | Blue | Tzadiel/Ruler |
| Geburah | Power | Energy | Red | Khamael/Warrior |
| Tiphareth | Beauty | Success | Yellow | Michael/Healer |
| Netzach | Victory | Personnel | Green | Haniel/Love |
| Hod | Splendor | Communications | Orange | Raphael/Teacher |
| Yesod | Foundation | Strategy | Violet | Gabriel/Fertility |
| Malkuth | Kingdom | Management | Olive | Sandalphon/Earth |

## The Tree of Life Pillars

| Pos./Active | Neg./Passive | Neut./Balanced |
|-------------|--------------|----------------|
| Chokmah | Binah | Kether |
| Chesed | Geburah | Tiphareth |
| Netzach | Hod | Yesod, Malkuth |

# Preparation

Think of using the Kabbalah for business as though you'll be attending the most revered and sought-after business and success seminar ever produced. It will include the greatest business lecturers—the likes of Bernard Baruch, Donald Trump, and more. It will also include the world's most renowned success gurus, from Napoleon Hill to Anthony Robbins. All of the greatest business minds will be at your disposal, because what you will be doing is tapping the cumulative knowledge of the entire business universe and pinpointing the exact knowledge you need.

The difference in using the Kabbalah is that you can prepare in your home office and never have to leave your easy chair to attend this mystical seminar. But you will have to get your mind into a magickal altered state unlike you've experienced in any business lecture (any altered state you've achieved in most business seminars would include a great deal of snoring, I'm sure). The good news is that this procedure is not unlike most methods of readying yourself for magick. And it's excellent practice and exercise for *all* magick.

What you will be attempting to achieve is getting your conscious, rational business mind working with your subconscious, creative problem-solving mind. When the two are in sync through the Kabbalah exercises, you can enter and "touch" the Sephira that holds the answers to your dreams. As it is with any magickal working, your area, your temple, your holy place of conjuring must somehow set the stage for your mind to expand and be altered in the direction you're seeking.

Because you will be using a specific Sephira, the colors associated with the spheres are good places to begin to prepare your magickal space. If the color is yellow, use yellow candles or cloths to cover your altar or table. Use as much of the color as you can, because this influence will set your subconscious mind to more readily accept the sphere's call. It is also advisable to have a Tree of Life glyph with your chosen sphere and its appropriate color that has been constructed by you. You could use an enlarged copy of the illustration on page 129, but by making it with your own hands, you will reinforce the energy that acts as your mind's trigger for entering the Kabbalah's astral plane. So take the time to make your own Tree of Life map; the act of creation of any kind works well with using the Kabbalah, considering that the system is a virtual *handbook of the creation of the universe.*

Begin entering the altered state by sitting quietly in your darkened room free of outside noise and be sure you won't be distracted for at least twenty minutes or so. Once you've established a quiet working environment and have prepared mentally, you want to get into the right mind-set of learning, absorbing, and making cognitive, rational, intelligent business decisions.

Close your eyes and feel your body relax, beginning with your toes and then working up your body, concentrating on your legs, then your midsection, your chest, your neck, and finally your head. At each area, contract the muscles and then release. Don't worry about the actual performance; the mental work is just as good as the actual flexing of the muscles.

Once you feel that your body is relaxed as best as possible, concentrate with your mind's eye by picturing a large red-orange ball or sphere. Start picturing it as a faint-colored ball and then gradually increase its color and density until you have a solid red-orange sphere (the color of power) floating about six inches in front of your mind's eye. Focus on the sphere and hold it in your mind. If you feel resistance, that's okay. Eventually your mind will come back to the sphere that's now embedded in your subconscious and will act as a trigger to open the portal to the Kabbalah. Continue your meditation and concentrate on the business aspect of your chosen spheres. If you chose the sphere Netzach and are seeking its corresponding attribute of victory in some business deal you're involved with, visualize the sphere granting you access to an incredible boardroom or university filled with experts, books, computers, and any other valuable business knowledge you can imagine. See the sphere opening doors allowing you entrance to this world of consummate business expertise.

## Identify Your Astral Assistant

In traditional Kabbalah workings, the magician will call on one of the archangels or deities to answer his questions and the mysteries of the universe. Asking Michael the archangel, for example, to predict the third-quarter profits for your company, or how you can get a raise from your stingy boss, may seem a bit trifling in the grand scheme of the universe. And in respect for the age-old reverence for the Kabbalah and its mysteries, we will continue to call on the gods to assist us in *Corporate Magick*. However, we will only ask for *direction* to other, more contemporary and worldlier beings who are concerned with our material world. For example, we may call on the angel Michael to provide us with an audience with Andrew Carnegie to ascertain some industrial knowledge, or ask to see Og Mandino\* for some sales help. Remember, *all* requests are possible through the Kabbalah, so do not hesitate to ask your Sephira and deity to provide what you need.

The angel/deity whom you choose should be the being that's been listed with the Sephira you've chosen from the accompanying chart. You can invoke other beings to aid you, but you should only attempt this after you have been admitted to the world of the Kabbalah through your sphere a number of times. You body and mind have to be in good magickal condition before you can wander the astral plane and call your own shots. Learn how to enter the plane first, and then experiment with calling on other gods.

## Work the Energy

The energies that flow through the universe are constant. The same energy that flows through your body flows through the cosmos. And the original source of that energy is still moving and creating everything in our lives. The Kabbalastic description of

\*Author of *The Greatest Salesman on Earth.*

energy is the force that originated from "Ain," or Nothingness, and then followed the Path of the Flaming Sword, worked its way down nine stages of different manifestations until it reached the mundane, physical world that we now know. The Flaming Sword is also the divine lightning that infuses magicians with the power of the Kabbalah during rituals.

Our thoughts produce this energy—our personal Flaming Sword. Think about how brain waves can be measured electronically and how we often can accomplish great feats if we just "put our minds to it." This energy is twofold: It exists in our conscious mind and also on the alpha level of our subconscious. When we meditate and release alpha energy that's then combined with our conscious energy, we create a powerful summoning tool better known as magick. And by focusing this energy through a road map like the Kabbalah, we open the gates to the mysteries.

In addition to creating energy through meditation, it is known that we can resonate that energy through sound—be it prayer, invocations, mantras, or what have you—which stirs the energies into a magickal frenzy, bolstering the magick. Orthodox Kabbalists resonate the names of the angels, deities, and also have a set of Hebrew "words of power" that aid in the use of the system. In *Corporate Magick,* we will substitute our own words of power and will be resonating them accordingly. Sound is energy itself, so it is more important to resonate the pitch and tone than the actual words we use. The sound stirs the energy; the word sets the subconscious mind.

Begin using the words describing the Sephiroth on the chart. If you chose Geburah, its meaning is "power," so you can begin by slowly and deeply chanting the word "power" over and over, all the while concentrating on the Sephira. Chant the mantra ten or twenty times, not only hearing it with your ears but also visualizing the letters of the word pulsing and growing full of energy each time you say it aloud. Replace the word with *your chosen word of power.* If you were seeking a new job, perhaps your word would be "promotion." You will then resonate the word "promotion" ten or twenty times until you can vividly see the sound of the word penetrate the sphere. You can effectively use any word of your choice after you invoke the angel/god name of your Sephira.

Once your conscious and subconscious are working in tandem, you will produce a direct energy that will begin to "soften" the sphere of your choice. Look at your Tree of Life poster and see how the divine lightning of creation bolted through the top of the Tree, charging each Sephira as it made its way down through the heavens—through the nine "Splendid Lights" and eventually to the tenth Sephira, Malkuth, the physical world. This is the same energy that is now surging through your very spirit. Once the energy has settled, you will feel a warming in your chest and hands. You are now prepared to make your journey as many mages have done in the past and are still doing today.

At this point you will see in your mind's eye how the Sephira is beginning to morph and change shape, becoming more and more malleable and less dense. The sphere is becoming primed for entry by your magickal body. The resonating sound of your mantra is now the key that ultimately pierces the sphere. Continue your chant until you see an opening begin to form on your red-orange sphere. It will begin as a pinpoint but slowly grow larger and larger until you can see a great brilliance of a white-gold light stream through the pinhole. This is your thought-energy, allowing you entrance into the world of the Kabbalah. Once inside, you are ready to ask the questions and receive the answers to all of your business inquiries.

## Ask for Help

Your first visit to the Kabbalah's astral plane may simply be a brief look at the environment. Some people see an Olympus-like temple with columns; others see great fields of nature and mountains; still others are in a comfortable room awaiting the entrance of a wise master. My experiences have always been in environments in which I feel most comfortable and which are usually awe inspiring. I feel that I am in a place of pure security and conducive to learning. If all you experience is a quick glimpse, don't despair: Your magickal mind is not yet prepared to absorb the immense amount of knowledge and fascination that awaits you. Be patient; it's the divine inhabitants' way of initiating you into the world of the Kabbalah.

When you have reached the inner realm, you will be met by beings created from energy and thought that have evolved over eons. Each Sephira has its own "gatekeeper" of sorts, which appear as images including kings, warriors, nude women, children, and more. You will be seeking your own deity whom you summoned, whether it is an angel or god. This being may not appear to be what you think—possibly with no wings or robes—or, he may look exactly that way. And when you reach other levels of attainment, your mentors will have the forms of great business leaders because those are the people from whom you are seeking answers. The important thing is that you begin to ask the questions that are important to you. If you don't receive verbal answers immediately, simply try to "feel" the answer with your mind. Use your intuitive sense and although you may not get a literal reply, your mind, your magickal "self," will pick up on the instructions through the melding of your conscious and subconscious minds. You may experience many unusual entities in the Kabbalah's realm, but keep focused on whom you are seeking. You'll know your mentor because he will also be seeking you. And when you are advanced enough to have identified your being as someone in the business world, your task will be that much easier. It's like having the eternal Executive Volunteer Corps at your disposal.

Don't be shy about your visit to this realm. If the beings you encounter are not comprehensible to you, ask why they have manifested themselves and if they are there to help you. Resonate your word of power or the word of your chosen deity toward any image you are not comfortable with. If it is not there to assist you, then it will disappear by virtue of your thought-energies. You will be met by many elements, images, and symbols. Concern yourself only with those that have some meaning to you. When you use a sphere to work the Kabbalah, it is analogous to entering a tunnel—you will encounter many things on the other side, but you'll have to direct yourself to what you need to know.

Almost two years ago, I wrestled with a publishing question that prompted me to ask the Kabbalah for help. I knew I had an idea for a book, but I didn't quite know what the concept would be until I worked some Kabbalastic magick. I visited with one of my business mentors, William Randolph Hearst, on the astral plane and spent what felt like hours discussing what my book would be and how I would present it to my agent. It appeared to me that I didn't get a solid answer, but Hearst did tell me that the word "corporate" is used as a contemporary catchall for almost all business in the United States. And of course I was writing a book on business "magick." The working concept and title miraculously occurred to me, and *Corporate Magick* was born.

It is important that once you have the results of your seeking, you act on them right away. Your thoughts—your energies—have been put into action at this point. If you recall a cornerstone of magick, "as above, so below," you'll understand that what has been given to you on the Kabbalah's plane is ready to be manifested here on the physical plane. If it's not used within a short period of time, the magick's energy will dissipate.

## Create Yourself as a Master

The last step in your Kabbalah training is perhaps the most beautiful. You will be re-creating yourself on two planes of existence: the astral plane and the earthly physical plane. Because you have now opened your subconscious mind and have allowed the energies of the universe to flow into your spirit, you have begun the process of creating a new you. Your physical body, your conscious mind, and your subconscious are melding together to form a powerful magician through the power of the Kabbalah.

At first you won't recognize very much difference in yourself, but after working the Kabbalah and honing your thoughts and wishes, you will begin to feel subtle changes. The lessons you learn through your spheres will take hold in your physical being and strengthen your mind. Don't let the experiences you received from your sphere be forgotten. When you are ready to confront a situation in the physical world, recall the power you felt from your sphere and let it course through you once again. What you are doing is reconnecting your magickal self with your physical self as a conduit for your desires.

If you asked for a promotion at work and have gotten advice from the Kabbalah, that new information is now part of you and it will add confidence to your request. Visualize the scenario beforehand and then, armed with your newfound power, talk to your boss knowing you have magick on your side. If you sought advice when confronting an adversary in some political office machination, you will now have the courage to defend yourself. The more you work the Kabbalah magick and massage the Sephiroth, the more magickal strength you will gather.

What's more encouraging, as a corporate magician you already have the knowledge of the business world at your disposal from everything you've ever experienced in your working life. Every bit of knowledge, circumstance, skill, tactic, and so on will be increased tenfold as the magick aids you. Each time you think a thought, that thought's energy will couple with your sphere's advice and bolster you as a magickal master.

Because you have now entered and experienced universal and divine powers, your whole persona will benefit, allowing you to actually shape and form a new person. Your ability to think more clearly in meetings will increase; your demeanor with subordinates and superiors will change, becoming more confident and assured. And, most importantly, you will realize that you've harnessed a great and wonderful aid in achieving whatever you want from your business career. By thinking positively, your thought-energy always had the ability to influence your reality. Now, with the added benefit of the Kabbalah's strength and infinite wisdom, anything is possible.

## INSTANT MAGICK INDEX CARD

### Using the Kabbalah

To tap into the magick of the Kabbalah quickly, follow these five steps:

1. Identify the Sephiroth of need—Malkuth (kingdom of the material) and Tiphareth (money and success).
2. Draw a cube with a cross (+) inside in black ink on a piece of amber-colored paper (Malkuth's color in the Assiah* world of action is black, and Tiphareth's is amber).
3. Meditate on the drawing and resonate on the god name "Adonai" and the archangel "Raphael" ten times each. Also resonate your power word ten times.
4. When you visualize your god, angel, or mentor in your mind, ask your question. You can also call on the *Corporate Magick* Cabal.
5. Visualize the divine lightning energy coursing though your body and end your meditation.

---

*The Kabbalah is also influenced by four distinct worlds of creation. *Corporate Magick* is concerned only with Assiah, the world of action.

# CHAPTER 9

# Tools of Your Trade—Candles, Herbs, and Incense Magick

Forget your computer, cell phone, briefcase, and personal digital assistant—for now, anyway. As a corporate magician you've already discovered that sometimes you will use your regular business accessories for magick, but you are also working with different, more mysterious types of tools—tools that until now have never even been considered applicable for the world of commerce and commercialism. They are the tools that have been on the dusty shelves of sorcerers for hundreds of thousands of years. They are the stuff of nature that's grown in the wild since the dawn of Wicca, the old religion. And they continue to this day to be simple, yet powerful, conduits for fantastic magickal workings.

As a corporate magician, you are in a very unique position in the world of magick. You are among the first breed of sorcerers who are melding the age-old practices and mystical arts with modern-day business principles to command results in your companies and your businesses. Candles, herbs, and incense, three elements indispensable to the practice of magick, have been tried-and-true ingredients relied upon by novices and masters alike. And now they're equally important to you. You've seen how candles give you meditative entrée to the astral plane where your magick is born. You've learned that herbs and incense are used for favors of the spirits and the gods and how ancient recipes can be used even now for powerful magickal results. Now, with the information that follows, you'll be able to master the use of this magickal trio and create customized spells for whatever business scenario you face. Using candles, herbs, and incense is wonderfully simple because you can use one, two, or all three in any combination you see fit. Remember, it is your magickal will that is the catalyst, and at this point in your practice you are ready to experiment with the vast array of ingredients at your disposal in occult shops, herbal stores, New Age shops, *botanicas,* and on the Internet. I encourage you to tap the universe without fear by using these tools. Let the flicker of the candle grasp your mind and open it to the wonder of magick. Allow nature's herbs to heal and stimulate your magickal being. And let the incense of the mystical masters permeate your inner sanctum as you breathe in their powerful scents. All these tools have a purpose and a particular task. You are the benefactor of volumes of study and practice penned in the most esoteric grimoires ever compiled. Use the knowledge at hand; it will work wonders for you, and your business life will never be the same.

# Candles

One of your most important and easy-to-use magickal tools is the candle. Candles are portable and easy to prepare for a spell of meditation, and they can be placed in your home or office. The core of the belief and power of candles stems from the fact that a candle's essence is "controlled fire," one of the first elements ever harnessed by humans and put to hundreds of uses, many of which were essential to survival of the species. So it's no wonder that this primal instinct is still very much within us, and a hidden key to unlocking our subconscious powers. The magickal power of fire—the reason we stare so intently at a burning flame—taps our very magickal core.

Historically, candles have been associated with both good and evil magick. There are the lunatic legends that candles are Satan's (Lucifer—the Angel of Light) special offertory and were made of human infant's fat for mythical black masses. There is also the tale of the "Hand of Glory" candle used for necromancy that's made of a dead man's fat, placed in his severed hand, and said to be impossible to remove. But candles also represent knowledge, life, and the light of the world in many religious ceremonies. As is true in all magick, the devices are nothing more than the means to direct the magician's will, and candles can be infused with positive or negative energy depending on the magician's intent.

Today you will find candles made of tallow (sheep's fat or lard) or, more commonly, bees wax, which come in every imaginable color, shape, and size. And there are a host of ready-made candles claiming to address every possible magickal desire. But by using a few simple combinations, the *Corporate Magick* system allows you to take advantage of age-old wisdom and work effective candle magick without remembering thousands of "prescriptions." Many occultists believe that a magician's power is more effective if he makes his own candles from raw materials, and it's certainly possible to find tallow or beeswax, prepare the raw materials, and freeze them for future use. Some claim that dressings adhere better to lard candles than wax, and thus provide stronger magick. But again, it's all about your willpower. The candles are the magickal conduit and your mind's vehicle.

A few things to keep in mind when working candle magick:

- Never blow out a magickal candle with your breath; use a fan or snuffer.
- Let a magickal candle burn out completely by itself before you dispose of it.
- Remember the proper "dressing" methods: Begin from the center, then dress toward the top for positive results, or toward the bottom for defensive spells.
- Once lit, candles should not be handled.
- Don't use previously lit or novelty candles for magickal purposes.

- Candles with cotton wicks are best.
- Use matches instead of lighters.

The inherent power of candles is based on their color, dressings (oils), and significant attributes and astrological correspondences. On page 151, there is a table of candle basics gleaned from vast numbers of spell combinations and geared specifically for business and success. As with all magickal workings, you must prepare yourself with the proper *Corporate Magick* affirmations—the six statements and three basic steps. Once you are mentally prepared, simply light the candle (dress with appropriate oil if desired), and envision the desired outcome in your mind while you meditate on the flame.

Use the candle chart as a guide to using candles in conjunction with the other magickal disciplines incorporated in the *Corporate Magick* system. But do not limit yourself to its descriptions. If you find a new oil that has worked in the past, combine it with a candle that best suits your goals. For example, if you are seeking to start a new business, you should use a red candle dressed with success oil. Although the candle draws its power from the astrological sun sign Aries, the person whom you're trying to borrow capital from may be a Taurus, so you'll want to use another candle to attract that power as well.

The list contains the oils that are most commonly found in occult shops and New Age stores and those that are known to be effective in the business scenarios listed, so it's a safe bet that your magick will work using what's listed. If you're so inclined, there are literally thousands of blends that can also be used, so you can mix ingredients to make your own. There are numerous books on the subject of magickal oils, and with a little help from your local occultist you can brew up a batch that serves you. (Contact me at www.corporatemagick.com if you find a new oil that's worked for you.) Remember, experiment with what works—it will strengthen you as a corporate magician.

## *Corporate Magick* Candle Magick

| Color* | Business Attribute | Astrological Symbol | Uses | Dressing |
|--------|--------------------|--------------------|------|----------|
| Red | Energy, aggression | Aries | Start-ups | Success oil |
| White | Knowledge | Cancer | Computers, information | Orchid oil |
| Green | Prosperity | Libra | Accounting, finance | Money-drawing oil |
| Blue | Experience | Pisces | Management | Control oil |
| Black | Defense | Capricorn | Security | Myrrh oil |
| Orange | Strategy | Scorpio | Planning, career | Lavender oil |
| Yellow | Persuasion | Leo | Sales | Gambler's oil |
| Violet | Ambition | Sagittarius | Expansion | Jasmine oil |
| Gray | Negotiation | Aquarius | Legal | Anise oil |
| Olive | Competition | Taurus | Partnerships | Sweetpea oil |
| Brown | Longevity | Gemini | Procedures | White rose oil |
| Rainbow | Production | Virgo | Manufacturing | Ginger oil |

*There are a number of other color candles, but those listed here are the basic magickal colors that correspond to aspects important to *Corporate Magick*.

Some occultists gauge the effectiveness of the candle magick by how the flame burns, how the candle melts, and how the candle's container is affected by the working. According to some Santeria candle interpretations, if a candle explodes it has prevented someone from attacking you, or if the candle has a low flame it means your work area is infected with negative energy.* Personally I've never witnessed a candle explode, but based on experience from a combination of other magickal disciplines where I have applied *Corporate Magick* principles to candle magick, this is how magicians should interpret a magickal candle's reactions:

Low flame—The magician needs stronger visualization.
High flame—Magick is working and was long overdue.

*From *Santeria: Candles, Herbs, Incense, Oils* by Carlos Montengro.

Burns out on its own—A spell is being launched at you.
Black smoke—Negative energy is being eliminated.
Flickering flame—Your goals are split; confine the magick to one wish.
Flame cracks container—Use stronger dressing.
Flame relights after extinguished—Call for help; you need assistance or a stronger spell.

# Herbs

Herbs are another set of tools that work well for *Corporate Magick.* A common magickal belief is that all things of this earth are influenced by the natural forces of the earth. As it is in the Kabbalah (see chapter 8), Malkuth, the Sephira that governs this world, manages all things of a materialistic nature, so when a magician wishes for prosperity or fortune through Kabbalah magick, his wishes are directed at Malkuth. And so it is with the use of magickal herbs. By virtue of them being naturally grown, they have a direct magickal influence on worldly goods. And of course, that's what we're most concerned with—our worldly goods!

An added benefit of using magickal herbs is that they're easy to find and prepare and fairly simple to use in most magickal spells. All these attributes fit perfectly with the pragmatic approach of *Corporate Magick.* The downside of trying to discern which herbs are best for what situation is that there are more than we could ever list in this book, much less in part of a chapter. So I have picked the ten most essential herbs for use in business based on a number of books, ancient spells, and lots of talking with like-minded business magicians. I also considered the availability of these herbs. Although most can be purchased on the Internet nowadays, there's always the question of potency and credibility. Always use your local shop first for magickal supplies; there you can touch and smell the ingredients to ensure freshness.

The list here includes the ten herbs you can use right away. Before using them, however, you have to empower the plants

## The 10 Essential *Corporate Magick* Herbs

| Herb | Business Correspondence |
| --- | --- |
| Buckthorn | Legal matters |
| Clover | Finances, accounting |
| Devil's shoestring | Career, employment |
| Dragon's blood reed | Defense, protection |
| High John the conqueror* | Success |
| Lovage | Sales |
| Mandrake root* | Management |
| Mugwort | Stock market |
| Snakeroot | Money |
| Sweet pea | Partnerships |

*Caution:* This herb is poisonous; do not drink.

with your visualization skills by launching your intentions into the universe. You can then either sprinkle the herbs around a candle in combination with candle magick spells, create a pouch or sachet, or infuse them in water and use them as teas. (Use a tea strainer filled with 1 teaspoon of dried herb, and pour boiling water over it. Let it steep for ten to fifteen minutes. *Caution:* Never drink poisonous herbs.)

Many of the herbs used in magick are also available as oils. For example, you can cut the stems of High John the Conqueror root, place it in olive, vegetable, or mineral oil, and let it soak for a few weeks.* It can then be used in the same manner as dried herbs. Now just follow the next few steps beforehand and work the *Corporate Magick*:

1. Physically handle each herb before your magick and "sense" its power. (If you're mixing herbs, use a wooden or clay bowl. *Do not* use metal.) Use the herb only if it "feels" right for your purpose.

*From *Cunningham's Encyclopedia of Magical Herbs* by Scott Cunningham.

2. Create a vehicle for the power, such as in a pouch or use as a tea.

3. Visualize your wishes while you hold the pouch, drink the tea, or sprinkle the herbs.

Once you've chosen the herb you want to use, selected the method, and activated it (performed your spell), the next big step is to . . . forget about it. The natural magick you have invoked dances, so to speak, only to the natural rhythms of the universe. Just as a wound will not heal before its time, magickal spells that are tied to nature also take their time. So sit tight and let the magick work at its own pace. You will not be disappointed.

---

## CASE STUDY
## SANDRA'S HERBAL ESSENCE

---

The use of magickal herbs in business is a lot more common than I even suspected. In one conversation with a young college woman named Sandra, an MBA student in Los Angeles, I was pleasantly surprised to learn that she has used magickal herbs to help her in her part-time business as a dog walker. She confided in me that the costs of her schooling were becoming too much to handle. She saw an opportunity in her neighborhood to walk dogs and started her small business.

"It wasn't long before I was making a few hundred dollars a week, and my business was taking on a life of its own," Sandra said. "I needed to either hire someone to help me or lose the money. I remembered how a class I attended on comparative religion spoke about Hebrew mystics who would use certain herbs in pouches to bring them wealth. I always had an affinity for magick—I'm very good at visualization—so I decided to find the herb, 'snakeroot,' and design a talisman of my own."

When I asked her why she resorted to using magick, especially herb magick, to help her fledgling business, she said that it seemed easy and naturally safe. "I wasn't 'spooked' by using herbs. After all, they're just plants. And I believe there's inherent power in Mother Earth, so I made the pouch, visualized my school bills being paid, and it helped—a lot. I now have two other students helping and sharing the wealth."

---

# Incense

The third tool of our trio of simple yet effective magickal assistants is incense, a favorite scent-producing material that has been a staple of the Pagan and Christian spiritual communities for thousands of years, yet only gained general popularity since the youth culture of the 1960s. The exotic appeal of its aromatic scents and the romance associated with distant and esoteric cultures has contributed to making incense an increasingly powerful aid in the New Age world. But in the magickal tradition, incense has been used for much more than a pleasant smell. The smoke of incense is an aid to help the magician focus his concentration, much like the flame of the candle. Its power also energizes and "charges" the surrounding air with the magickal will of the practitioner. It was thought by ancient wizards that the magician's breath contained his life force—his energy—and that breath melded with the smoke of the incense disappeared into the universe, where it would take the form of a magickal imp, and then do the magician's bidding on the astral plane.

The magickal power of incense is also closely related to another magickal staple—the four elements. The burning of incense affects three of these elements: the earth (usually the natural ingredients of incense—herbs, resins, barks); the air (smoke rises and becomes a part of the air); and fire (the burning sets the magick free). Incense, especially in religious ceremonies, has also been used to protect against evil spirits and purify the air for divine communication. In Islamic cultures, incense is burned to ward off the "evil eye," and Christian masses regularly purify

their altars and conduct vesper services with incense to consecrate churches and funerals.

The simple act of smoke being created, seen, inhaled, and
then disappearing, is a basic, yet very profound magickal representation. Subconsciously it allows the magician to feel as though
the powers of the elements are at his control and his magick is at
its peak. The primary use of incense in the *Corporate Magick* system is to bolster this feeling so that it strengthens your magickal
abilities, while at the same time relaxing your senses so they are
laser sharp. The fumes of the incense are a means to alter your
consciousness and allow your magick to flow. And because the
use of incense requires so little preparation and action, you as a
corporate magician can concentrate fully on directing your will
toward your business desires.

The beauty of incense is that it can be used as an adjunct to
any of your spells or rituals to enhance the working, or you can
use incense alone as the catalyst for simple spells. And all it really
takes to begin using incense as part of your magickal works is to
secure a censer in which to ignite the incense. You then place a
piece of charcoal in the censer, or sand in the case of a metal
thurible, which remains hot to keep the incense burning. Censers
can be commercially produced incense burners that are made in
hundreds of forms from human skulls to elaborate gold urns. Or
you can use a ceramic or stone plate that will not burn. For
*Corporate Magick* purposes, I suggest that you use something
representative of your career if possible. For example, if you are
an accountant, perhaps you can find a novelty ashtray or flat
paperweight adorned with dollar signs. Better yet, use an item
emblazoned with a company logo as a censer to burn your incense. The continued reinforcement of your business position
will help your magickal power, and is yet another manifestation
of sympathetic magick.

Of all of the magickal tools and elements available, whether
you use incense will be determined a great deal by your own personal preferences regarding smell. As with herbs and candles,
there are myriad types of incense to choose from, not only in
their pure state but also in infinite blends—many customized by

magicians out of pure preference of aroma. And that's a very good reason to choose a type of incense, because the mental effect it has on the magician is very important. If you don't like the smell, it will distract you from your magick regardless of whether it has particular magickal properties that are perfect for your working.

In the interest of simplicity and to provide you with a fast and effective way to use incense the *Corporate Magick* way, I have narrowed your incense choices to what I feel are the ten most applicable and relatively easy to find types for business and career based on my experiences and the experiences of many working corporate magicians. The list is a basic primer and a starting point. You certainly can use only one incense for a spell, but your magick will be most effective using a combination. So if you are doing a spell to obtain money, you can blend money-drawing incense with patchouli (for attraction) to strengthen the working. I encourage you to try different blends not only for the resulting power you will see in your magick, but also because you will become better acquainted with the many types of incense and will have the basic knowledge to create *exact* blends for any business situation.

Incense can also be mixed with oils, so if you cannot find a particular incense in its original form you can substitute the same oil and burn the incense and oil together.

It's worth noting that incense can be a very powerful "suffumigation" (smoke that rises upward) aid in place of actually casting a spell. The vapors of the incense are said to capture spirits and negative energies and pull them up and out into the air, thus purifying the environment—sort of like a natural ionizer. In fact, there is a school of occult thought that links the use of incense with astrological movements and the planets and subscribes to the theory that the planets "pull" the vapors of the magickal incense, so for incense to work they have to be in tune with the correct planentary correspondence. Of course it couldn't hurt to explore this method (Francis Barret's early-nineteenth-century classic *The Mage* lists these correspondences). But I have personally found incense to work without consulting the stars. In fact, this method can come in handy in a number of office and business settings. In places where your magick must be concealed, incense can be burned under the guise of making a place smell good when the real reason is to perform its magick. You'll find that this ruse can work wonders, especially if you are attempting to rid your workplace of someone bringing you harm. Simply use a protective or banishing type of incense and let its vapors spread through the air. Your nemesis will never know what hit him.

### 10 Essential Types of *Corporate Magick* Incense

Most incense comes in the form of cones, blocks, sticks, or dried powders.

| Incense | Business Correspondence |
| --- | --- |
| Benzoin | General business prosperity |
| Bergamot | Career, personnel |
| Clove | Finance, accounting |
| Cinnamon | General success |
| Frankincense | Solve problems, legal |
| Ginger | Attract investors |
| Lemon balm | Increase sales |
| Peony | Longevity, insurance |
| Myrrh | Progress, technology |
| Sandalwood | Increase business |

## CASE STUDY
## BILL'S SWEET SMELL OF SUCCESS

My friend Roger's son Bill, who had just graduated from college a few years before, was working on Wall Street as a fledgling broker and was sharing a condominium apartment on the Upper East Side of Manhattan. Most people who know the area would agree that there's not much to complain about living in this swanky area of the city, besides perhaps some small apartments and noisy neighbors. But Bill was having a hard time, mainly because two of his roommates at the time worked in businesses that required them to dine out almost every night and entertain a great deal. If one of the roommates wasn't rolling in at 3 A.M., the other was serving guests cocktails and playing music all night long. For Bill to make the hour-long commute to his job and be at his desk by 9 A.M., he had to get to bed by midnight.

So when Bill's roommates announced that they needed more space and wanted to sell their shared condo, Bill couldn't wait. But the market was slow and buyers were scarce. Knowing of his father's magickal proclivity, Bill decided to seek some mystical help from his dad as a last resort. Roger told me that he advised Bill to begin with simple incense magick just to get him accustomed to focusing. Incense, Roger thought, was not foreign to young people and a good way to get Bill initiated without a lot of training.

Bill welcomed the advice and went about burning sandalwood incense, which is known to help along real estate sales. Bill magickally prepared himself one evening while his roommates were out. Sitting alone in the dark, he burned the incense in a special censer given to him by his dad. As the fumes filled the room with a sweet fog, he envisioned lines of people waiting to see his apartment all with checkbooks in their hands and clamoring for him to "make a deal."

Well, to Bill's dismay no one showed up days or even weeks later. And in a last-ditch attempt on a rare night when he was again alone in the condo, Bill tried his incense again. Within a few minutes after burning the herbs, a loud knock came on the door. It was his upstairs neighbor, complaining that the smell of the incense had somehow leaked through Bill's ceiling and was permeating the neighbor's apartment. Bill apologized, and he and the neighbor struck up a pleasant conversation. It just so happened that the neighbor, who was at this point starting to enjoy the mystical aroma of the incense, was looking to buy larger space in the building because his daughter was moving to New York and taking his upstairs apartment.

The upshot, Roger recalled, was that Bill sold his apartment, met the neighbor's daughter, and they were married in two months' time. It may not have been the way Bill thought the spell should have worked . . . but it *was* magickal nonetheless.

## INSTANT MAGICK INDEX CARD

### Triple Spell for Business Success and Guidance

1. Secure a green candle, High John the Conqueror herb, benzoin incense or oil, and an incense censer.
2. Mix the John the Conqueror herb and benzoin incense/oil in a bowl and let dry.
3. Sprinkle the mixture around the base of the candle; during a waxing moon, burn the incense mixture, wait ten minutes, and then light the candle.
4. Concentrate on the candle flame and ask the universe for success.
5. Invoke the name of the *Corporate Magick* Cabal three times and ask for guidance.

# CHAPTER 10

# How to Be a God at
# Your Company

Congratulations. You have the power. Whether you have mastered the principles of focusing your will and sending your energy into the astral plane or you've simply worked some basic candle magick, you have begun the journey that only the courageous and bold have attempted. You have taken steps to use a very powerful ally—the universe—in your business life and career. And now you must use this power to its fullest by establishing yourself in the workplace as "one of the wise," a keeper of hidden secrets—by all measures a true corporate magician.

But learning the mysterious methods of real magick, unlocking the hidden secrets of the greatest sorcerers who ever lived, and being able to take the pearls of occult wisdom from ancient and venerated grimoires to use in your business and career success is only the groundwork for becoming a true corporate magician. As effective and practical as the *Corporate Magick* system is, you've learned thus far that it's *you* who are the catalyst that makes the magick happen. Just as a great athlete will first learn a sport, then excel, and eventually bring his own special ingredient to his performance, so will the magician. Call it style, confidence, arrogance—it really doesn't matter. It is the essence of greatness, and it's what makes a person stand out from the crowd, become an idol, and command awe wherever he appears. People stop and stare, want to be near, and often giggle and act childish, which they would normally never do with "regular" people.

A great deal of this charisma has to do with what the person has accomplished in the past and his documented successes. But many people are very accomplished in their respective fields, yet don't have that "superstar" attraction. And this mysterious quality is not simply a product of physical beauty or vast intelligence—there are many average-looking film stars who are considered mega earners, and average celebrities who have written books, hosted TV shows, or sung hit songs, yet they are considered "divine" by everyday people. What is this special gift? What makes two equally talented people vastly differ in their greatness? Is it personal charisma alone? Well, it *is* charisma, but not charisma that was a genetic gift. Most people are not born to greatness. The answer is simply that who these mega stars are *perceived* to be is what sets them apart. And the innate confidence they hold in their minds and bodies shines through and creates the perception. It is magick that makes them gods.

And so it is with the corporate magician. It is a well-known fact in the occult world, especially in disciplines that employ sympathetic magick like witchcraft and voodoo, that spells often rely on the spell target's *belief* that a charm will work as much as on the will of the magician and the energy of the universe. If the magician displays unfaltering confidence in his abilities, the people around him will pick up on this strength and will believe he is the holder of a unique quality *they just can't put their finger on.* Of course, there always will be those who think anyone interested in the occult, much less practicing it, is a kook. I maintain that most of the folks who react that way are really frightened of what they don't know and think magick is evil knowledge forbidden by their traditional religious conditioning. The remaining skeptics who claim that working magick is just nonsense have a right to their opinion, but we know better. And we prove it on these pages in each testimonial and case study of working people who have successfully used the mystical arts.

Whether it is in your office, your store, or anywhere you do business, what you want to do to bolster your effectiveness as a magician is to create an air of mystery and wonderment that can be perceived by everyone around you as something supernormal. Many of the greatest magicians of our time utilized great magickal "spin" (and without the help of professional "spin doctors"). These mages would often boast of their magickal accomplishments to anyone who would listen, and despite the true effectiveness of their magickal deeds and actions, they were thought of as great sorcerers and wizards. This is not to say that their magick didn't really work; it's just human nature to embellish stories of fame and greatness. And if it creates the right perception among people, then that perception takes on a life of its own. That's how legends are born.

Where magick is concerned, it is even more beneficial to cultivate a darker and more mysterious air because of the nature of magick's occult (read: "hidden") practices. People are much more intrigued by what they don't see rather than what's blatantly visible. One of the most notable—albeit maligned—magicians of the twentieth century, Aleister Crowley, went as far as "spinning" himself into "Beast 666," and was commonly referred to as the "wickedest man alive." Well, you don't want to take your image *that* far, of course, but if you are in a position where being up front about practicing the mystical arts is your intention, you *do* want people to know you have hidden knowledge. It will give you that much more credibility when you work your magick.

"Outing" yourself magickally, so to speak, carries even more benefits than simply changing people's perception of you. Because you have now added another dimension to your personality and constantly release your "I am a magician" energy into the universe, your magickal will becomes that much stronger. Like-minded individuals will seek you out, as will those in need. In addition to boosting your ego, you will boost your magickal being. Because you are now establishing yourself on the earthly plane as a magician, your magickal counterpart is becoming stronger. In effect, you are doing twice as many magickal workouts, so you will reap twice the benefits. You will no longer be a part-time magician, but now an adept at your craft.

Your new persona as a magician will transcend your regular self, and you will begin to feel more confident and appealing. Think about how you have felt after you've accomplished some arduous task or handled a difficult situation. Once it was over, your spirits soared and you felt invulnerable. And I'm sure people around you commented on how good you looked or your sense of newfound confidence. Whenever I've experienced a business success, no matter how minor, my peers sensed my accomplishments and within minutes would begin to seek my advice and coaching. My confidence level rose, and everyone in my proximity felt the energy. This is the same energy that is born out of your will as a magician, and that you send into the astral plane to do your magickal bidding, but it's now manifested in your earthly personality. And you will feel this power as well. Your status as a magician, by virtue of your rituals and spell casting, now shines through. You exude a new sense of wisdom and occult power that most of your business associates will experience, and you will notice an increased amount of respect from everyone with whom you do business. "Deep calleth unto deep; there is a natural affinity in all men's souls for that which is half hidden in a twilight world, and once you have gained the attention of a person's deep mind, you may then proceed to work on it, using your own as a broadcasting unit for your wishes. This is the essence of witchcraft."*

The biggest drawback to your new stature as a magician is that the people who know you practice magick might think you odd, crazy, or downright evil. You must decide whether to go public with your powers based on a number of factors that only you can know. Many corporate magicians, because of the sensitivity of their jobs and companies, are very clandestine about their practices. But this doesn't mean their new inherent power is

*From *Mastering Witchcraft: A Practical Guide for Witches, Warlocks & Covens* by Paul Huson, page 27.

not evident. It may be less pronounced, but it will continue to be felt by others.

In contrast, there are those, especially in the creative fields, who flaunt the fact that they practice the occult arts. As New Age and the occult have gained popularity over the last decade, some of the stigma has lessened. In fact, interest in magick, especially in Wicca and after-life experiences, has flourished, so to hear that someone may be a practicing witch nowadays may still raise some eyebrows, but most people won't be running for the holy water. In the business world, magick's less likely to be accepted, but the nice thing about business is that it likes success. As magick continues to prove that it can be a practical tool to make money and vault careers, then, magicians will become that much more a part of the norm. And as testimonials to *Corporate Magick* continue to prove that magick is a viable business tool, more and more corporate magicians will enter the workplace.

So let's assume you are prepared to let the world know you have the secret powers of *Corporate Magick* at your disposal. There are three basic areas you should address to create your corporate magician persona and the perception that you possess occult powers. They are your office or your store; your clothing and jewelry; and your magickal demeanor.

## Your Magickal Office

Nothing screams "success" and "corporate privilege" like the size and placement of a person's office. Corner-office space is a legendary benchmark of power and prestige and the bone of contention in myriad company political battles. But as corporate magicians, we're more concerned with what our office conveys to our associates than with where it's placed or what it signifies in the company. After all, we possess a higher knowledge, and if we don't have that cushy space right now, we'll get it within time. In the late 1970s, Michael Korda wrote a best-selling book called *Success!* wherein he laid out, among other successful techniques, the "Successful Office," with advice on how to place furniture, styles of decor, and even the ethnic and personality "type" of office that would work in particular kinds of companies. For example, he talked about the "WASP" office, the "jock" office, and so forth, and how each should be created to convey success.

In *Corporate Magick,* we go about creating our magickal office in a less direct way. Sure, we're concerned about gaining success, but we know that the means to it is through magick, and we're attempting to create a different perception of our power. So instead of following the typical lead as mapped out in books like Korda's, we want people to look at our work space and get the impression that we are learned wizards who are mavericks with a mission. That being said, each magician must determine how blatantly he wants his office space to convey his magickal bent. As I've already pointed out, the creative fields may be open to having pentagrams and voodoo symbols displayed, but banks may not. This also raises the question of religious tolerance, and company policy must be taken into account. Some firms have strict policies about any display of religion of personal preference, so use some discretion when creating your office environment.

However, if you are at liberty to show the world you're a magician, I've narrowed down office environments into three categories—Proud Magician, Mysterious Magician, and Private Magician—each with varying degrees of magickal display.

## The Proud Magician's Office

For the corporate magician who has no personal qualms or company restrictions about telling the world that he practices magick, the proud magician's office should convey an air of mystery and a heavy sense of hidden knowledge. It is the full-blown, all-out sanctum of magick for the corporate magician who throws all caution to the wind. This type of office will probably be feasible only in very progressive and, perhaps, "edgy" companies, likely in the entertainment and advertising fields. Of course, if it's your own business, then you can do pretty much whatever you like, so your office decor is limited only by your imagination.

The proud magician's office should be painted in earth-toned colors, preferably greens, reds, and browns (*no* white walls), and kept light enough just to be able to conduct business. There should be drapes on the windows, or the blinds or shades should be drawn at all times. Sunlight should be kept out, and there should be no fluorescent lighting of any kind. All lighting should be provided by small lamps and candles (if permitted by fire codes). Furniture should be heavy woods and ornate fabrics. Leather seating is good, as are mahogany chairs or sofas. What you want to convey here is an air of occult knowledge in a kind of "spooky," but not scary, atmosphere. Think Sherlock Holmes's study with a touch of Harry Houdini.

An essential aspect of the proud magician's office is the display of books. The more books and bookcases you have in your office, the better. And needless to say, titles about the occult, magick, witchcraft, the strange, and the supernatural should all be prominently displayed. In fact, selected titles like *Magick in Theory and Practice, The Mage, The Magician's Companion, The Grand Grimoire* (and of course *Corporate Magick*), along with any title with the words "spells," "charms," or "hexes," should be placed on your desk so as to be easily read by anyone sitting directly in front of you.

Items or icons such as statues, posters, and incense censers should also be placed in your office in strategic places where they will attract attention. Statues of gods or occult symbols that decorate your space impart to visitors that you know the secret significance of these symbols, and therefore must know how to use their power. A well-placed statue of Pan, the half-man, half-goat god of pleasure—if for nothing else but his appearance and traditionally erect male member—is a lively conversation piece. Likewise, any symbols of witchcraft or even astrological symbols evoke the magickal mood that reinforces your image as a magician. A strategically placed ceremonial hooded robe hung on the back of your office door or on a coat rack is also a nice touch.

Another useful way to convey magick is the burning of incense. The exotic aroma of incense—besides being a mood-inducing agent in itself—is a perfect backdrop for a "supernatural" workplace, especially blends of Roman Catholic altar incense (available at religious supply stores) and frankincense.

A word of caution when preparing your office or work space: don't get hokey. Cheap Halloween decorations, rubber bats, wands, and too many "scary" books or candles scream that you're "trying too hard"; you might be considered simply eccentric rather than enlightened. So use discretion. You don't want to be Harry Potter, but you do want to be magickal, so use authentic items that you find at occult shops and items you actually use in rituals. You'll find they make for better conversation than tchotchkes and are legitimate devices through which to impart your *Corporate Magick* wisdom.

If you happen to work in or own a retail store or business and you are the person in charge, you will undoubtedly adjust all of the above to your clientele. It's advantageous to you to have a workplace that conveys "magick" if it will somehow improve your image and influence the people you are dealing with. You may want to impress a salesperson with your prowess, or you may have customers who think it's chic to have a magickal shop-keeper. And if you own a New Age or occult store, *botanica,* or psychic advisory, the sky's the limit. These suggestions hold true unless you happen to be self-employed or work from your home, in which case your environment can be furnished simply to enhance your magickal personality.

## *The Mysterious Magician's Office*

The mysterious magician is much less blatant about his position as an occultist for any number of reasons, which may include the conservative nature of his company or industry, or the mere fact that he is more comfortable not "showing off" his abilities. Nonetheless, he may want to at least present a mysterious air and hint at the fact that he knows the ways of the sorcerer. For the most part, this kind of work space would include items of an occult nature, but be much less apparent. For example, occult books can be intermingled on bookshelves with other types of books but strategically placed so people will notice them. Statues and icons can be placed in corners discreetly. Early in my career, I worked in a company on Wall Street. I had nothing magickal in my office at all except for a few tribal masks from Mexico hanging on my wall, which represented anthropology rather than the occult. Still, these few masks became a constant conversation starter and a perfect entrée for me to discuss my magickal prowess with whomever I wished.

Unlike the proud magician, the mysterious magician's office should be less dark but still lit with only lamps. Natural light should be kept at a minimum. The goal is to subliminally alert people to your *mysterious* environs, but not put them off with an ominous effect. Furnishings are less important here because the overall effect is less "in-your-face." A gothic chair somewhere in the corner, again as a conversation piece, or perhaps a crystal ball or large red or black candle—all are the kind of furnishings that the mysterious magician can use to effect in his personal corporate sanctum. Once any of these items are noticed by visitors, you can then take the opportunity to hint at your predilection for the occult. As the conversation continues, you can gauge whether or not to divulge your secret knowledge. The air of mystery that you will exude will create curiosity among your coworkers, having them always wondering what you're really all about.

## The Private Magician

The private magician's office is virtually free of any occult symbols or identifiable works. The watchwords for this magician are "discretion" and "subtlety." An occult book placed next to a book on anthropology or psychology is okay, as is an esoteric painting of a mythical scene or mysterious foggy moor. Or, you may display an interestingly "unique" statue, perhaps of a shaman or Roman god. These subtle furnishings will work. Whatever gets the message across without screaming "magick" is fine. In the classic lighthearted film about witchcraft *Bell, Book and Candle,* the main-character witch was the proprietor of a shop that sold magickal tribal statues, but from the street, no one, not even her main love interest, could discern that she was a witch from the appearance of her store.

Another clever method to get the message across is through music. Play music by the group Enigma, Gregorian chants, or what's sometimes called "Dark Wave" music by bands from the specialized Projekt record label. You'll also find a host of New Age recordings available—from Buddhist chants to siren songs—which can also be used as ambient background.

You may ask how someone can benefit at all from being so quiet about his abilities and knowledge. Isn't the idea that corporate magicians should cultivate their image so as to gain respect and gather energy for their spells? Well, the benefit lies more in what's communicated by the private magician *before* anyone enters his office. This is done by the magician's demeanor and well-placed conversation. Once someone's curiosity is piqued, the subtle placement of magickal accoutrements within the office then become apparent to the visitor in a sort of "Oh, now I get it" moment. The result is the same; it's just that the method is more discreet.

## INSTANT MAGICK INDEX CARD

### The Magician's Office

**Proud magician.** Obvious occult books, statues, and symbols. Dim lighting; heavy furniture and drapery (no cheap Halloween decor). Incense and candles.

**Mysterious magician.** Subtle occult displays; some natural light. Some New Age books, "moody" paintings, small candles, tribal masks.

**Private magician.** Virtually no *apparent* occult symbolism. A few books, possibly a nondescript magickal statue or symbol.

# Clothing and Jewelry

The days when just about everyone knew what was meant by "proper business attire" are over. What with "casual Fridays" and a much more relaxed approach to workplace individuality, personal preference has come a long way. Yes, banks and more conservative businesses still require suits for ladies and gentlemen, and depending upon your profession, you may be faced with some sort of uniform requirement. But a major element of establishing your image as a corporate magician is based on your clothing, so you need to modify your wardrobe as best you can to convey the message you want to deliver. That all-important first impression goes a long way. Let it be known that you are a wizard in business clothing.

I have broken down the business world's clothing requirements so we can adjust your magician's clothing appropriately. You are probably employed in one of three areas of business that have loosely defined clothing "rules": liberal, relaxed, or conservative. And once again, if you are self-employed, your attire is totally up to you. But if you're not, you will be expected to conform to the status quo to some extent. What you want is for your peers to be aware that you are a student of the occult, making your magick that much more powerful within your company or with your clients.

## *Liberal Magickal Work Attire*

Let's start with the easiest area in which to establish your magickal attire—the liberal businesses, which include the creative, entertainment, and artistic worlds. In these types of offices, almost anything goes fashionwise, and it's almost beneficial in some cases to be edgy and on the fringe of clothing styles. So to establish yourself as a magician requires only that you wear clothing and jewelry that symbolize the magickal arts. What does that mean? Well, you probably don't want to go to work in a hooded robe (although I have seen witch friends wear long woolen robes in public in the winter months in New York, to no one's surprise).

Wear clothing that can be considered eccentric and in line with magickal preconceptions. This can include a lot of black clothing, "gypsyish" dresses for women, and, of course, any garment that makes a literal or graphic statement. Many self-proclaimed "goth" types who are sympathetic to magick if not practitioners themselves center entire wardrobes on shirts and accessories that include pictures of goth bands, magickal luminaries, and spooky comic characters. Your taste may not accept clothing of that kind, and that's fine. What I'm suggesting is that if you wear clothing already associated with the occult, you've already won half the image-creating battle. And yes, much of what's available is hokey and geared toward teenagers. But even in youth-oriented retail stores, you can find items that look magickal yet not cheesy. I would stay away from Anne Rice T-shirts, but a symbolic pentagram can work. Flowing black dresses are good, but I would avoid skull-and-crossbones jackets. You get the picture; make it mysterious, but not ridiculous.

## Relaxed Magickal Work Attire

Establishing your magickal image in this environment is a little trickier than in a progressive workplace because chances are, you will have a diverse mix of people and managers with different ideas of what is and isn't acceptable. The watchword here is "regular" clothing—accentuated with the mysterious. For example, you may wear black suits every day, but with different-colored shirts and ties. Eventually people will notice that you always wear a black suit and wonder why, but it doesn't set off the "kook" alarm. If asked, you can explain that it's part of your magickal makeup. I actually used this method in a former publishing job; when asked, I simply said that most members of the clergy wear black clothes, and my religious convictions center on magick. My response set the stage for many stimulating occult conversations and a wonderfully interesting time in my career.

Fashion accessories are a staple of the magician who is in a relaxed work environment. An interesting long dark coat, a wide-brimmed hat, unusual glasses, and sunglasses can all be used to set yourself apart from the ordinary and establish an air of occult knowledge. You can exercise more latitude at certain times. For example, on certain witch's sabbats like Beltane (May 1), you could wear a deep red shirt that's in sharp contrast to your normal color scheme. When asked, mention that you are celebrating the Wiccan rite of spring.

Use jewelry to add another dimension to your image, especially if your clothing leans to the conservative side. If you are in an environment where sports shirts or blouses are permitted and you have clothing that has subtle occult symbols sewn in as adornments or patterns, that's fine also. Look the part of someone who has an affinity for magick and the occult, but don't be conspicuous. Your mysterious persona will shine through.

## Conservative Magickal Work Attire

This is the toughest wardrobe to pull off and still have people get the impression that you are a mage. You must be much more imaginative than your fellow magicians who work in more accepting fields, and yet meet the approval of the powers that be. Your task is to be even more subtle about what you wear than your "relaxed" environment counterpart. One trick is to be consistent about one piece of clothing that is inconsistent with the conservative majority. That sounds contradictory, so let me explain. If, for example, you wear a pocket handkerchief as your peers do, wear a red silk pocket square every day. If you wear a woman's business suit with your hair pulled back, wear a black kerchief around your neck daily. Sooner or later your trademark will become noticed, and no one will know its purpose—unless of course they ask. Then you can launch into a discussion of your "secret" power, and from that point on your reputation will spread like wildfire without your ever having to buck the fashion police.

Of course, jewelry will work wonders in this arena as well. Wearing a lapel pin that is obviously esoteric in nature on all your outfits is a stronger statement and actually will stand out more on a conservative suit than it would on a more blatantly magickal outfit. If you can't find a pin that symbolizes your particular magickal leaning, check with local occult shops and ask if they will make a customized pin for you.

A unique woman's bracelet can also create the same effect. Many practitioners of voodoo and Santeria wear colorful bracelets that are immediately noticeable—but unbeknownst to their business associates, these women are often expert occultists working in the guise of American corporate executives.

## *Jewelry*

Choose rings, bracelets, pendants, pins, and earrings that make definite statements. Despite the fact that they are not always immediately noticed, as are your clothes, people *do* notice what you're wearing on your hands, ears, and wrists. In fact, once a personal meeting occurs, most people will scrutinize your adornments carefully. Think about how many times someone has commented on your "nice watch" or "beautiful ring." When you wear something that's a little odd or offbeat, it will be noticed even more. Regardless of your outfit, make a point of wearing at least one piece of jewelry that makes a magickal statement. There are myriad possibilities available from New Age and occult shops, on the Internet, and even in everyday jewelry stores. A psychic friend of mine found a zodiac charm in a strip mall that's unlike anything she's ever seen. Many times local artisans will sell their wares to small shops, so look for the unusual that says "magick." You never know where you may find a treasure.

Interesting jewelry is also a great conversation starter, especially if it signifies your magickal bent. Most people know what a pentagram looks like, but they don't know the number of different definitions of the magickal star. A half-moon always gets an inquisitive look, and signs of the zodiac are natural icebreakers. Wearing occult jewelry is tantamount to wearing a lodge ring or professional association pin—it makes a clear statement to others.

And where magick is concerned, it gives you yet another way to establish yourself as a magician.

Another benefit of wearing magickal jewelry is that its effectiveness applies to all industries because it can be blatant or subtle. The well-known Wiccan can wear her pentagram necklace proudly everywhere she goes, and the Wall Street Wiccan can wear her pentagram pin or ring as well. Jewelry allows you to regulate the amount of your magickal image you want to expose at any given time.

## INSTANT MAGICK INDEX CARD

### Dressing for Magickal Success

**Liberal workplace.** No limit to your magickal attire. Wear black or colorful flowing garments, tasteful literal T-shirts, eccentric whimsical outfits. Occult and symbolic jewelry.

**Relaxed workplace.** Be subtler. Pick a consistent style and accentuate regular clothes with magickal accessories. Use jewelry that makes a magickal statement.

**Conservative workplace.** Don't stand out, but create a mystique. Wear one consistent occult accessory or piece of jewelry to evoke interest.

## Your Magickal Demeanor

Your clothes, office, and accessories are important parts of your magickal image, but nothing is as crucial in establishing yourself as a corporate magician as your magickal demeanor. Your demeanor transcends what you would normally think of as your regular business personality. And we all have business personalities. We have a work self and a regular self. Our work self acts more professionally and is usually on guard for corporate predators and sharks in the business waters. Our regular self is who we are outside the business environment—our interests, our families, our magickal life. What is important to remember as a corporate magician is that to establish yourself as a master of the mystical arts in business and gain the awe and respect that comes with this label, you must merge your regular self with your business self. You must keep in mind that to work your magick, you must be a magician first and a businessperson second. And to effectively transfer that attitude and project that vibe into your workplace, it's imperative that you keep a frame of mind that constantly reinforces your self-image as a magician. I cannot stress enough how crucial it is that you *think* magickally when at work, because your thought-energy will create an aura around you that others will sense. I guarantee you that if you are true to your own self-image as a master magician, the power of your mind will shine through. And each time you strengthen your earthly position as a magician, your astral entity, your cosmic adept, also becomes stronger.

I've just mapped out how your office and clothing contribute to your magickal status, but you can disregard all of these ideas if your demeanor—your magickal charisma—is intact. You simply won't need them if your will is powerful enough to grab your colleagues' attention. The right office and clothing will, of course, aid in how you're perceived, but the way you carry yourself magickally is the key to the complete corporate magician. If you are able to project an aura of mystery, hidden knowledge, confidence in magick, and an unfaltering *belief* in the power of magick, then everything else will fall into place. Walk into a room of 1,000 skeptics with the pure faith that magick works (and you know it does—the proof's on these pages) and you can convince 999 of them that magick is real.

Keep in mind that you will not have to change your personality. You can continue to be the person you've always been—gregarious, intellectual, and introspective. That part of you doesn't change. What changes is your mental image of yourself. You are now a magician, a wise person, a seer, a sage, someone who understands, appreciates, and uses the mysteries of the universe to make things happen in accordance with your will. The simple task of holding this image of yourself in your mind will cause an initial shift in your outward appearance, and everyone around you will feel your presence. It sounds very simple, but it works. Think wholeheartedly as a magician and you *become* a magician. Once the change in your mental image occurs, you will begin to be approached by people who are drawn to your mysterious makeup for reasons of curiosity, to gain knowledge, or simply to challenge you because they think you're odd. This is where your outward demeanor must take charge and the pragmatic part of your training as a corporate magician must kick in. You have created an air of mystery by virtue of your mental image, office, and/or clothing. You need to cultivate that mysterious quality and back it up with knowledge about magick. You must have answers to people's questions, but by the same token, you must also be somewhat vague. Your goal is to tease those outside of the magickal world with sexy and perceived "forbidden" knowledge so they never really know everything about you. Be intriguing, but a bit hidden. If someone asks a question about the occult or whether you practice magick, answer in generalities at first until you are comfortable that this person is sincerely exploring the arts. Note the following examples:

QUESTION: *What's with all of this spooky stuff? Do you really practice black magick?*
POSSIBLE ANSWER: You know, *black* magick really doesn't exist. It's up to the spell caster. But I know some spells that really work.

QUESTION: *I heard you have used magick to get ahead at work. Is it true?*
POSSIBLE ANSWER: Lots of hard work, some luck, and an occasional spell work wonders!

QUESTION: *Someone told me you could help me increase sales using magickal potions. Can you help me?*
POSSIBLE ANSWER: I once had a lucky amulet given to me by my

grandmother that I used to help me sell things. There are a lot of things I can show you that can help bring fortune your way.

Of course, your response will be based on your own personality, but an answer that doesn't deny the question and piques further curiosity is your goal. Such a response creates an air of mystery. It says, "This person [you] knows about this magick stuff," and it begs for more information. This approach strengthens your magickal demeanor without putting people off.

You will also be faced with situations where magick becomes the topic of conversation in office groups or perhaps parties attended by your business associates. It's at this time when you can expound upon what you know, and, if you feel comfortable, how you work magick. People will undoubtedly ask for parlor tricks, and unless you know some sleight of hand, avoid entertaining them. If you do know some tricks, make it clear that it's stage magic; the real thing is a lot more interesting.

As a corporate magician, you will often be walking a thin line between respect and being ostracized in business. Many will think you're evil, while others will simply think you're kooky. Still others will think you have profound knowledge of hidden secrets and they will attempt to latch onto you, with a mind toward turning your power against you for their own gain. Deal with each individually, and trust only your faith in the magick you know you can perform. Make it clear to your allies that you can help them in times of need, and make it crystal clear to potential enemies that you possess ways to defend yourself beyond their wildest dreams.

There may also come times when your interest in the occult becomes an issue with your superiors, or possibly people in business who are very religious and are frightened by your stance. I have found that the best way to deal with these problems, if pressed, is to simply explain that magick is an avocation of yours that you've studied over many years and have had an interest in since childhood. This says that you don't deny being a magician and at the same time dissuades any fears. If objects in your office become objectionable, take them out. At that point, your standing as a practitioner has already been established; the fact that it's being taken so seriously may actually benefit your magickal presence, establishing you as a de facto "god" at your company.

## INSTANT MAGICK INDEX CARD

### Cultivating the Magician's Demeaner

1. Keep a constant mental image of yourself as a master magician.
2. Maintain a "mysterious" air through clothing and personal effects.
3. Answer questions about magick vaguely, but open-endedly, until you are comfortable with the person who is inquiring.
4. In serious magickal discussions, know what you are talking about.
5. Handle skeptics and troublemakers with an air of hidden knowledge.

CHAPTER 11

# What They'd *Never* Teach at Harvard Business School: The Author's Personal Story

**P**eople often ask me what good all the magick I've learned is if it doesn't work in the real world. They say that I could have studied analytical theories on management in any good MBA program and provided my boss with an impressive chart on macroeconomics in an effort to get ahead. They reason that the key jobs would get done and I'd probably get the raise and the promotions like most hotshot executives. But there's a flaw in that argument: If every MBA who walked the streets were expert enough to get ahead on academics alone, we'd have a country full of CEOs. There wouldn't be "street smarts" books about business like Mark H. McCormack's *What They Don't Teach You at Harvard Business School* and Harvey Mackay's *Swim With the Sharks Without Being Eaten Alive*, to name just two. The point is that the occult techniques in *Corporate Magick* go far beyond anything that can be learned in school. Business street smarts are of course valuable, but as we've learned so far, there exist even more potent methods of achieving success that go far beyond conventional wisdom. That's the whole premise of this book and the core of its philosophy. The cynics who "pooh-pooh" magick's effects may take issue with its power, but what follows is *my* personal, hard example of how I used business acumen, street smarts, and magick to attain some pretty lofty positions and hefty compensation.

Of course, I cannot discount any talent, skill, or luck that also played a part in my scenario, but I could not have accomplished it all without the use of magick. What I am certain of, as are almost all of my colleagues in *both* the business and metaphysical worlds, is that hard work and luck are not the only elements in business success. A great deal of intuition, coincidence, and serendipity—occurrences that aren't measurable and concrete and often happen without explanation—influence our careers. But unlike most people who just take these gifts for granted or don't bother with what they can't explain, I chalk it up to magick.

*I had a major problem at the very apex of my corporate career. I was faced with a pivotal situation at my company, a consumer magazine publishing house, that would set the stage for my present livelihood and probably the remainder of my working days. Although I had successfully performed other workings and spells in the past to get myself out of hot water and secure promotions and salary increases, I knew that this would be a major challenge to my magickal abilities. The results were not only very successful, but also what I now see as my crowning magickal achievement. It's what made me a corporate magician supreme. These special workings reinforced my belief in the value of magick in business so much that I look at them as the epiphany that actually sparked me to write this book. I used magick in a special way and couldn't have asked for a better lesson in American management.*

Although few people would have looked at the fact that I rose through the ranks of a publishing company from a lowly assistant editor to a vice president in a few years as a problem, I faced a series of circumstances that not only were upsetting to me personally, but directly endangered my career. My "corporate back" was often against the wall in New York City, a place where being tough is a prerequisite for getting out of bed. And in the creative fields, competition and backstabbing reach their peak. So when my hard work and diligence paid off and I was in a position I enjoyed, I thought things were good. But petty jealousy and envy are often right around the next cubicle, so when some dubious colleagues decided that they would do me in, I knew it was time to put magick to work.

Although my responsibilities as vice president and editorial director were centered on the creation and publishing of magazines, the advent of "new media" and the Internet vaulted the company into a brand-new arena and potential profit center that was predicted to be the hottest opportunity in years. With my background in computer journalism, I was tapped by senior management to consult on the new Web site development operation.

The department created to focus on providing Internet services and Web sites had actually become a major profit center over a very short period of time. In fact, it became so profitable that it appeared as though this department would make more money than the actual publishing operation, which had been the core of the company since it began some twenty-five years before. The division had grown so large it was having serious growing pains. And the problem was exacerbated because it was being managed by technical and creative types, who are traditionally notoriously bad managers. The newly designated managers found themselves wrestling with issues of new technology, a burgeoning department, and little direction.

Two of the managers who had equal ranking within the department began a turf war of sorts that at first escalated and eventually died down over a few months after the weaker manager capitulated under fire. Both were creative types, but the victor had a much stronger penchant for control and was flamed by an extremely healthy ego. During their short battle, the de facto manager just about ate up his rival and spit him out. He thus became the acting head of the department, virtually running it as he saw fit. Eventually his rival had enough, and to no one's surprise submitted his resignation to the top brass. But this left a management void and a creative hole at the top of a department that also needed some serious help. It was a situation where the company management had to step in or be faced with a disastrous situation and the potential loss of huge profit.

I'd heard in the rumor mill that the stronger of the two supervisors had actually requested that I step in to replace his missing counterpart, but at a lower level. I knew I didn't want to go into this department at the same level as either of the players, much less at a lower position—in the company hierarchy, this wouldn't even be considered a lateral move. My goal was to run the department.

As a manager, I appreciated the value of a juicy rumor, but I needed hard information. As a magician, I decided I must hear for myself, and without direct confrontation the only alternative was to use magick. I'd have to find out where the rumors started and what was on management's mind.

In the past I'd used magick to travel the astral plane. Astral projection, as it is sometimes called, requires a great deal of visualization and concentration, but the basic skills are very much the same as performing most magick, so I was well prepared. I realized that traveling the astral plane was the only way I'd hear firsthand what the decision makers were contemplating. If all went well, I would have all the ammunition I needed to work subsequent spells and achieve my goals.

I'd decided to approach my working in a three-step manner. The first step required that I tap my subconscious mind, and following the path of many mages before me, I would first meditate and prepare my mind for engagement on the "other side." This preparation would then open the doors and allow my mind to become a conduit to the universal paths. Second, I would mentally create the actual environment on the astral plane. This required exacting visualization, calling on every one of my senses to create the room I'd magickally visit. Once the room was created with sight, smell, sound, and touch, my spiritual counterpart—the inner adept—could then be an eyewitness to how the interactions would commence.

Once all of the astral preparation was complete, I could then enter the ethereal realm and, based on the results of my experiences, prepare the proper workings to bend reality in my favor. As already mentioned, magick very much depends on "as above, so below." So what I could change and influence on the magickal plane of existence would then directly affect the physical world.

If you recall earlier chapters, any serious working should include a good deal of mental and physical preparation. And although hours and hours of that kind of preparation for the regular corporate magician is unlikely in today's harried world, astral projection is so intense that a dedicated mind is necessary. The astral traveling ritual can be very personalized, but the end result must relax your mind and prepare your body for exhausting strain. I knew my preparation had to be especially targeted because whenever I summoned my inner adept, it required an enormous amount of focused concentration and attention to detail—above even regular astral projection. As the inner adept, I was attempting not only to travel to another dimension, but also to actually resolve a problem by absorbing all of the available information. It was tantamount to climbing a mountain and counting and remembering each rock you pass on the way up. My innermost subconscious mind had to be in order to get a clear handle on the whole situation. In effect, I had to become a magickal Jedi.

At home I readied my magickal chamber with specially prepared incense, proper mood lighting, and music to assist me in going deep within my magickal mind. Ritual and items of magickal significance always enhance my workings, and in this case my "inner sanctum" had to contain fully charged tools. The atmosphere had to reek of deep devotion to the task at hand, so my favorite incense burned, mood music was on the CD player, and candles provided the room's only light. Once the chamber "settled"—that is, it absorbed the daily vibrations and sanctified the area—I began the preparation with a simple summoning chant of my own making based on primitive rhythmic tribal chants that allowed me to open my mind to reveal what I'd already heard or was exposed to but didn't consciously realize. My main concerns were my financial prosperity within the company and my ability to be happy in what I was doing, so I composed this basic rhyme with those goals in mind:

> *My work, my world*
> *Reveal and unfurl*
> *What lies in the way*
> *Of riches and play*

The chant rings of Wiccan rhyme, but it holds with my idea of using many esoteric teaching for my ultimate purposes. I chanted this mantra over and over. As magician Aleister Crowley said, "Invoke often. Inflame thyself with prayer," and that's exactly what I did, intoxicating myself with my goal so that nothing could stand in my way. After about twenty minutes of stillness, my mind took flight into the astral plane. I was out of my physical body, and the ensuing results were astounding. My intense meditation and visualization was so focused that it created a Kabbalistic magickal portal that appeared to me as a large mahogany door with gold inlay. I could sense a rumbling of voices on the other side of the door, and for a moment was a bit frightened over what might lie on the other side. I have never experienced such a vivid astral trip—I attribute it to the fact that my very well-being was at stake, so the whole magickal process was intensified.

Passing through the door, I was in the presence of the company executives and managers, all of them involved in conversation or at odds with each other in a workplace environment that exactly mimicked our corporate settings. The machinations of the executives hit me like a bolt of lightning and allowed me to learn the plans I'd desired firsthand.

As I circled the room in the astral plane, I heard people's opinion of the situation and what they thought of the other managers and myself. You must realize that this wasn't imagination running amok. What I experienced was tantamount to actually sitting unnoticed in a room full of people. I could hear what they were saying and, more importantly, see their reactions to each other's comments—it was as though I was reading their minds. This was completely accomplished by my meditation and visualization. It's similar to what's been recounted by students of Jose Silva's "Mind Control" techniques, where within the alpha state of meditation the practitioner creates a "room" of familiarity in his mind that he can visit at will. What was different was that my magickal training focused my will much more intensely and with a clear purpose in mind.

What I heard was disturbing. Management was considering me for a lateral move—not what I wanted at all. Their decision was based on not rocking the corporate boat, but in my mind, it was based more on a lack of firsthand knowledge on their part. After what seemed like hours, but in real time was only about ten minutes, I regained my conscious state and grounded myself from the astral trip by taking some fresh air and eating a hearty meal. But my mind was on fire from the revelation, and I realized what I had to do—my direction was clear.

My next step as a magician was to convince my superiors that I was the person to be put in charge before they started considering their erroneous options. As I've stated earlier, a magician must decide well before his workings how he is going to proceed. The choices are to strike in defense, or ignore your foe and bolster your own power. I chose the former. As a magician under fire, I wasn't prepared to just sit back.

My initial plan was simple because I wasn't concerned with doing my superiors any harm—I just wanted to coax them a bit—so I chose to start with simple candle-burning magick, which has always proved a reliable magickal catalyst. I began the candle rituals on the days of the waning moon (three days before the full moon to ensure power and draw influence toward my workings) and started with two simple candles: a purple candle designed for influencing people in high places, and an orange candle for smooth business dealings. The colors are an essential part of sympathetic magick and help channel the magician's thoughts and will. The color purple is regal and affects those in power, while orange is serene and an excellent choice for getting out of sticky situations. Both candles were prepared with special "influence" oils and carved with my superiors' names. I used the candles as conduits for my wishes, concentrating on the flames and once again honing my own will—the magician's cardinal practice.

To strengthen the entire working I secured a green seven-knob candle (see chapter 9) to represent money, and dressed (anointed) it with success oil, starting from the middle of the candle and rubbing upward and then downward until the entire candle was dressed. I concentrated on the flames and directed my thoughts so the president and senior vice president thought more highly of me than ever, peppering the projections with illustrations of my past accomplishments. It was my magickal resumé, burned into their minds through the power of the magick candles.

In the days that passed after I completed my workings, I felt strangely relieved and empowered all at the same time. I had worked magick many times before but I had never felt so exhilarated as after this bout with the universe. I was more attuned to what was happening in the workplace, and my peers commented on my newfound confidence. The magick was working through my body and spirit and even infusing my department with its power.

The desired results were achieved within about a week of my magick. I was asked to a meeting with my superiors, told of the situation at hand, and asked if I would like to join the department in question. Because I knew the results beforehand, I was ready to propose that I not just join the department but be put in charge. I made my case that my rival was inferior, lacked the necessary respect from his subordinates, and was not a team player—all points that had been brought up during my astral visit. More importantly, I laid to rest any doubts management had about my abilities, pointing out my accomplishments and plans for the new department. The magickal influence worked. They not only agreed that I should run the department, but also gave me the title I requested and agreed to a substantial increase in salary.

Of course, all of this could possibly have happened without my workings, based on ability and my track record in the company. But I was the one who presented the title and raise suggestion because of *what I already knew*. It's not likely that they would have offered me such a large package. The doubters may say magick didn't get me the promotion, but I know better, and I firmly believe it not only helped, but also got me a lot more in the bargain.

As successful as this working was, it turned out that it was only half the battle. My transfer into the new department threw me into a lion's den, because the surviving manager didn't exactly greet me with open arms. In fact, in our first few weeks of working together animosity grew under a veil of camaraderie and cooperation. It was evident that this manager resented my presence and couldn't get over the fact that I was his superior in a department that he felt he'd built. It was getting ugly, and I couldn't perform my job the way a department head was required to. It was again time to conjure.

Because I knew there would never be a way of working together in this situation, I decided that my rival would have to go. Any senior manager in any company knows that simply complaining about a subordinate (which technically this person was) is nothing more than a sign of weak management ability, and ultimately wouldn't get him ousted. My alternative was to have other people within the department—four key supervisors—expose his shortcomings and call for his termination.

Once again I engineered influence with a combination of magickal tools beginning with candle magick over the course of two months. I directed my focused will on each supervisor through the candle flames until I began hearing them, one by one, complain about the manager in question. At the same time I used a combination of spells that began with writing my nemesis' name on parchment, which I then burned, buried, and mentally tossed into the ether. I also made a poppet doll resembling him that contained a piece of his favorite pencil, which I'd managed to take from his desk. The poppet was designed to create some disturbing havoc in his life by being prodded, torn, and placed in precarious circumstances. It was manipulated in a way that inflicted mental discomfort, not physical pain. After all, I wanted him out of my hair, not to be harmed. By manipulating the poppet, I managed to create minor personal difficulties in his everyday life so he wouldn't be able to focus on his work, which included a major project of his that had a fast-looming deadline. The combination of his distractions and my supervisors' complaints set the stage for the final blow.

Machiavellian tactics aside, I knew that using magick to have him eliminated could have created some unsettling karmic consequences for me, but I had heard of many instances where he had badmouthed me to peers and superiors and was in fact engineering his own coup. In my mind I was defending myself, negating any worry about retribution. All magick is for gain of some sort. It's all in the approach of the magician's will; the universe will ultimately decide what is and isn't an act of evil, so my conscience was clear.

Once again in my private chamber during the subsequent full moon with my black cat Szandor at my side, I prepared what I knew would be the culminating spell. Short of consulting the darkest grimoires at my disposal, including *The Grand Grimoire*—considered one of the blackest of black magick manuals—I conjured an elaborate ritual within a protective circle of nine feet in circumference (a standard magickal size). Using the spells for strategy and career advancement (see chapter 3), I prepared a potion oil called "boss fix" from ingredients found at a local occult shop. This potion is designed to eliminate a nagging boss, and although my nemesis wasn't officially my boss, he believed he was, which gave him the mental position I needed to neutralize. I added a little extra protection by keeping nearby a jacinth stone, which is known to bring prosperity.

Keep in mind that previous to this working, I'd nurtured a "spooky" image within the department and the company. By virtue of this demeanor, which included my esoteric books, statues, and the overall ambience of my office, I created the picture in my adversary's mind that I was a practitioner of the mystical arts. His own belief that I *could* be a magician was his own demon working against him—a powerful ally for any magician—before I actually did anything.

The boss-fix oil was spread in his work space and eventually found its way onto his person. Havoc ensued.

Within a few days my target began experiencing personal problems—he had a flat tire on his way to an important meeting, his child's school called complaining about his son's minor disciplinary problems, his accountant suddenly lost some important paperwork he needed for a tax audit, and to top it all off, he lost his wallet. What with all of these distractions, my rival found it extremely difficult to focus on his job. The department supervisors became more and more displeased with him, and he eventually fell behind in his deadline. The final blow came when the supervisors, disgusted with his ineptitude, approached me one morning demanding that he be relieved from his position.

I subsequently set up an interview with senior management explaining that the key people in the department were calling for this person's head, and although I'd often voiced my displeasure with him, it appeared as though I had nothing to do with their revolt. In my bosses' eyes, my hands were clean. Senior management met with the supervisors, who railed consistently about the man's shortcomings and poor management techniques. By the second week of my working, he was fired.

The magick had worked. The spells did their job, and his own personal demons distracted him to the point where my magickal defenses took over. He had, in effect, hung himself by his own malevolent actions and suffered the magickal consequences of doing battle with someone who had a little help from the astral plane.

# Appendix: Resources

## How-To Tips

### *Make Your Own Magickal Oils**

Add 2 tablespoons of your chosen herbs or powders to 2 ounces of base oil (olive oil, mineral oil) or dipropylene glycol. Mix in a bowl (mortar and pestle) and store in a bottle for three days. On the fourth day, check to see that the oil has absorbed the mixture's scent. If its weak, strain the oil through cheesecloth and add 2 more ounces of oil. Add more mixture or flowers if desired. Store for three more days.

### *Customized Candle Dressings*

Add chosen oils, herbs, and powders to 2 tablespoons of base oil, mix, and store in a glass jar. One to 2 tablespoons should suffice as a dressing.

*From *Charms, Spells & Formulas* by Ray T. Malbrough.

## How to Dress Tallow (Lard) Candles*

Rub chosen oils and herb mixtures thoroughly on candles. Place in a plastic container and freeze until ready for use.

## Handmade Beeswax Candles†

Heat 2 pounds of beeswax in a metal pan. When melted, add your chosen herbs and powders. Stir well, and turn off the heat. After ten minutes, add your chosen oils and mix. Anchor a cotton wick to the bottom of a glass container and pour in the substance.

## Poppet Dolls‡

Cut two pieces of cloth in the outline of a human figure approximately six to twelve inches in length. Sew the two pieces together but leave the top open to add ingredients (herbs or powders). Mark the poppet with distinguishing male or female characteristics and whatever is easily identifiable (adding hair or eye color, for instance). Also include any business logos or signs that are appropriate.

# Information Sources

Hands down, the most complete resource currently available in book form is the revised and updated edition of *The Modern Witch's Complete Sourcebook* by Gerina Dunwich, Citadel Press. It lists books, magazines, stores, courses, a who's who, and more.

## Internet

Despite the instantaneous changes that occur on the Web, a must-have book for Internet resources is *The Wiccan Web*, Citadel Press, by Patricia Telesco and Sirona Knight.

---

*From *Santeria: Candles, Herbs, Incense, Oils* by Carlos Montenegro.
†Ibid.
‡From *Buckland's Complete Book of Witchcraft* by Raymond Buckland.

Needless to say, any good search engine will turn up thousands of sites. The following are but a few gems that I have discovered, with links to thousands of other great sites. And of course there's www.corporatemagick.com.

**General History**
www.religioustolerance.org

**Wicca**
www.witchway.net

**Satanism**
www.churchofsatan.com

**Kabbalah**
www.digital-brilliance.com/Kab/fag.htm

**Astrology**
www.astrology-online.com

**Voodoo**
www.voodooshop.com

**Supplies and Books**
www.poto.com
www.magusbooks.com
www.azuregreen.com (soon to be AbyssDistribution.com)

**Psychic Stock Picks**
www.marcusgoodwin.com

# Mail-Order Supplies

## *Herbs*

Aphrodisia
282 Bleecker Street
New York, NY 10014

International Imports
P.O. Box 2010
Toluca Lake, CA 91602

Azure Green
P.O. Box 48-WEB
Middlefield, MA 01243

# Recommended Reading

Many of you may be new to the world of magick and the occult sciences, so I have listed the basic books that I feel will give you a sound foundation with which to begin your *Corporate Magick* career.

## *Wicca*

Buckland, Raymond. *Buckland's Complete Book of Witchcraft*. St. Paul: Llewellyn Publications, 1991.

## *General Magick*

Conway, David. *Magic, An Occult Primer*. New York: Bantam Books, 1973. (May be out of print, but worth the hunt.)

Gonzales-Wippler, Migene. *The Complete Book of Spells, Ceremonies & Magic*. St. Paul: Llewellyn Publications, 1997.

Paulsen, Kathryn. *The Complete Book of Magic & Witchcraft*. Rev. ed. New York: Signet, Penguin Books, 1970.

## Solid History of the New Occult

Holzer, Hans. *The New Pagans*. Garden City, NY: Doubleday Books, 1972. (May be hard to find, but well worth the search.)

## Business Magick

Dolnick, Barrie. *The Executive Mystic*. New York: Harper Business Books, 1998.

Goodwin, Marcus. *The Psychic Investor*. Holbrook, MA: Adams Media Corporation, 2000.

Hendricks, Gay, and Kate Ludeman. *The Corporate Mystic: A Guidebook for Visionaries With Their Feet on the Ground*. New York: Bantam Books, 1997.

## Candle Magick

Riva, Anna. *Candle Burning Magic*. Los Angeles: International Imports, 1990.

## Herbs

Cunningham, Scott. *Cunningham's Encyclopedia of Magical Herbs*. St. Paul: Llewellyn Publications, 2001.

## Oils and Incense

Dunwich, Gerina. *Magick Potions: How to Prepare and Use Homemade Incenses, Oils, Aphrodisiacs, and Much More*. New York: Citadel Press, 1998.

## Voodoo

Turlington, Shannon R. *The Complete Idiot's Guide to Voodoo*. Indianapolis: Alpha Books, 2002.

## Santeria

Gonzales-Wippler, Migene. *Santeria: African Magic in Latin America*. St. Paul: Llewellyn Publications, 1997.

## Astrology

March, Marion D., and Joan McEvers. *The Only Way to Learn Astrology: Basic Principles*. San Diego: Astro-Analytic Publications, 1976.

## Kabbalah

Cicero, Chic, and Sandra Tabatha. *Experiencing the Kabbalah*. St. Paul: Llewellyn Publications, 1997.

## Satanism

LaVey, Anton Szandor. *The Satanic Bible*. New York: Avon Books, 1969.

# Bibliography

Adler, Margot. *Drawing Down the Moon.* New York: Penguin Books, 1979, 1986.

Ahmed, Rollo. *The Black Art.* New York: Paperback Library, 1968.

Andrews, Ted. *Psychic Protection.* Jackson, TN: Dragonhawk Publishing, 1998.

———. *Simplified Magic: A Beginner's Guide to the New Age Qabala.* St. Paul: Llewellyn Publications, 1997.

Argenti, Paul A. *The Fast Forward MBA Pocket Reference.* New York: John Wiley & Sons, 1997.

*Ars Notoria.* Seattle: Trident Books, 1977.

Ashley, Leonard R. N. *The Complete Book of Magic and Witchcraft.* New York: Barricade Books, 1986.

———. *The Complete Book of Spells, Curses and Magical Recipes.* New York: Barricade Books, 1997.

Atkinson, William Walker. *Mind Power, The Secret of Mental Magic.* Chicago: Yogi Publication Society, 1940.

Bing, Stanley. *What Would Machiavelli Do?* New York: Harper-Collins Publishers, 2000.

Buckland, Raymond. *Buckland's Complete Book of Witchcraft*. St. Paul: Llewellyn Publications, 1991.

Castenada, Carlos. *The Teachings of Don Juan: A Yaqui Way of Knowledge*. New York: Washington Square Press, 1968.

Cavendish, Richard. *The Black Arts*. New York: Perigee Books, 1967.

Cicero, Chic, and Sandra Tabatha. *Experiencing the Kabbalah*. St. Paul: Llewellyn Publications, 1997.

Clark, Peter J. *The Sorcerer's Handbook: Real Magic at Your Fingertips*. New York: Sterling Publishing Company, 1970.

Conway, David. *Magic, An Occult Primer*. New York: Bantam Books, 1973.

Cooper, Phillip. *The Magickian*. York Beach, ME: Samuel Weiser, Inc., 1993.

Crowley, Aleister. *Magick in Theory and Practice*. New Jersey: Castle Books, 1991.

Cunningham, Scott. *Cunningham's Encyclopedia of Magical Herbs*. St. Paul: Llewellyn Publications, 2001.

Dolnick, Barrie. *The Executive Mystic*. New York: HarperCollins Publishers, 1998.

———. *Simple Spells for Success*. New York: Harmony Books, 1996.

Drew, A. J. *Wicca for Men*. New York: Citadel Press, 1998.

Dunwich, Gerina. *Exploring Spellcraft*. Franklin Lakes, NJ: New Page Books, 2001.

———. *Magick Potions: How to Prepare and Use Homemade Incenses, Oils, Aphrodisiacs, and Much More*. New York: Citadel Press, 1998.

———. *The Modern Witch's Complete Sourcebook.* New York: Citadel Press, 2001.

Eason, Cassandra. *The Handbook of Ancient Wisdom.* New York: Sterling Publishing Company, 1997.

Gonzales-Wippler, Migene. *The Complete Book of Spells, Ceremonies & Magic.* St. Paul: Llewellyn Publications, 1997.

———. *A Kabbalah for the Modern World.* St. Paul: Llewellyn Publications, 1997.

———. *Santeria: African Magic in Latin America.* St. Paul: Llewellyn Publications, 1997.

Goodwin, Marcus. *The Psychic Investor.* Holbrook, MA: Adams Media Corporation, 2000.

Gordon, Leah. *The Book of Voudou.* Hauppauge, NY: Barrons Educational, 2000.

Greene, Robert. *The 48 Laws of Power.* New York: Penguin Books, 2000.

Hendricks Gay, and Kate Ludeman. *The Corporate Mystic: A Guidebook for Visionaries With Their Feet on the Ground.* New York: Bantam Books, 1997.

Hewitt, William W. *Hypnosis for Beginners.* St. Paul: Llewellyn Publications, 2000.

Hill, Napoleon. *The Master Key to Riches.* New York: Ballantine Books, 1965.

Holmes, Ernest. *The Science of Mind.* New York: Penguin Putnam, 1938.

Holzer, Hans. *The New Pagans.* Garden City, NY: Doubleday Books, 1972.

Hubbard, L. Ron. *Dianetics: The Modern Science of Mental Health.* Los Angeles: Bridge Publications, 1950.

Huson, Paul. *Mastering Witchcraft: A Practical Guide for Witches, Warlocks & Covens.* New York: Perigee/Berkley Publishing, 1970.

Jones, Laurie Beth. *Jesus CEO*. New York: Hyperion, 1995.

K, Amber. *True Magick, A Beginner's Guide*. St. Paul: Llewellyn Publications, 1990.

Korda, Michael. *Success!* New York: Ballantine Books, 1977.

Kraig, Donald Michael. *Modern Magick: Eleven Lessons in the High Magickal Arts*. St. Paul: Llewellyn Publications, 1992.

LaVey, Anton Szandor. *The Devil's Notebook*. Venice, CA: Feral House, 1992.

————. *Satan Speaks*. Venice, CA: Feral House, 1998.

————. *The Satanic Bible*. New York: Avon Books, 1969.

Mackay, Harvey. *Swim With the Sharks Without Being Eaten Alive*. New York: Ivy Books, 1988.

*Magic Charms From A to Z*. Middletown, RI: The Witches' Almanac, Ltd., 1999.

Malbrough, Ray T. *Charms, Spells & Formulas*. St. Paul: Llewellyn Publications, 1999.

Maltz, Maxwell. *Psycho-Cybernetics*. New York: Pocket Books, 1960.

*Man, Myth & Magic: An Illustrated Encyclopedia of the Supernatural*, Vols. 3, 10, 11, 20. New York: Marshall Cavendish, 1970.

March, Marion D., and Joan McEvers. *The Only Way to Learn Astrology: Basic Principles*. San Diego: Astro-Analytic Publications, 1976.

Mather, George A., and Larry A. Nichols. *Dictionary of Cults, Sects, Religions and the Occult*. Grand Rapids, MI: Zondervan Publishing House, 1993.

McCormack, Mark H. *What They Don't Teach You at Harvard Business School: Notes From a Street-Smart Executive*. New York: Bantam Books, 1984.

Mickaharic, Draja. *Practice of Magic: An Introductory Guide to the Art.* York Beach, ME: Samuel Weiser, 1995.

Montenegro, Carlos. *Santeria: Candles, Herbs, Incense, Oils.* Plainview, NY: Original Publications, 1994.

Murphy, Dr. Joseph. *The Power of Your Subconscious Mind.* New York: Bantam Books, 1963.

*Mysteries of the Unknown: Psychic Powers.* Alexandria, VA: Time-Life Books, 1987.

Nelson, Felicitas H. *Talismans & Amulets of the World.* New York: Sterling Publishing, 1998.

Paulsen, Kathryn. *The Complete Book of Magic & Witchcraft.* Rev. ed. New York: Signet, Penguin Books, 1970.

Reed, Ellen Cannon. *The Witches Qabala: The Pagan Path and the Tree of Life.* York Beach, ME: Samuel Weiser, 1997.

Riva, Anna. *Candle Burning Magic.* Los Angeles: International Imports, 1990.

———. *Golden Secrets of Mystic Oils.* Los Angeles: International Imports, 1990.

Robbins, Anthony. *Unlimited Power.* New York: Fawcett Columbine, 1986.

Roberts, Wess. *Leadership Secrets of Attila the Hun.* New York: Warner Books, 1985.

Rose, Donna. *Money Spells.* Hialeah, FL: Mi-World Publishing Company, 1994.

Rosenthal, Allen M. *Your Mind the Magician.* Marina del Rey, CA: Devorss Publications, 1991.

Rubin, Ron, and Stuart Avery Gold. *Success @ Life: A Zentrepreneur's Guide—How to Catch and Live Your Dream.* New York: New Market Press, 2001.

Sagan, Carl. *The Demon-Haunted World: Science As a Candle in the Dark.* New York: Ballantine Books, 1996.

Silva, Jose. *The Silva Mind Control Method*. New York: Pocket Books, 1977.

Smoley, Richard, and Jay Kinney. *Hidden Wisdom*. New York: Penguin/Arkana, 1999.

Spence, Lewis. *An Encyclopedia of Occultism*. New York: Citadel Press, 1993.

Suster, Gerald. *Hitler, Black Magician*. London: Skoob Books, 1981.

*The Grand Grimoire*. Seattle, WA: Trident Books, 1996.

Turlington, Shannon R. *The Complete Idiot's Guide to Voodoo*. Indianapolis: Alpha Books, 2002.

Tyson, Donald. *Ritual Magic*. St. Paul: Llewellyn Publications, 1992.

Whitcomb, Bill: *The Magician's Companion*. St. Paul: Llewellyn Publications, 1998.

Worth, Valerie. *Crone's Book of Charms & Spells*. St. Paul: Llewellyn Publications, 2000.

Wright, Elbee. *Book of Legendary Spells*. Minneapolis: Marlar Publishing, 1974.

# Index

Abraham, 15
Absolute concentration, 24–25. *See also* Sixth sense
Acacia oil, 122–23
Accessories. *See* Clothing; Jewelry
Accounting
  case studies, 69–70, 78–80
  clove incense for, 158
  clover for, 153
Adams, Evangeline, xviii, 76
Adler, Margot, 5–6
Advancement
  author's experience, 181–88
  bergamot incense for, 158
  *juju* for, 99
  Kabbalah for, case study, 131–34
  spell casting for, 48, 56–57
Affirmations, xxiii–xxiv, 23–24
African Yoruba tribes, Santeria and, 9
Age of Aquarius, 88–89
Agwe, 96, 98
Aida Wedo, 98
Air
  astrology and, 21, 83
  incense and, 155
Altars (altar space), 51, 97
  preparing, 33–38
Amulets, 61–63, 71–72
  case study, 72–73

for creativity block, 112–13
  definition of, 62–63
  Instant Magick Index Card, 73–74
  for spells, 45
Angels, 12
  Tree of Life and, 16, 131–34, 140
Animal sacrifice
  Santeria and, 9, 10, 106, 119
  voodoo and, 96–97
Anthony, Saint, 110
Aquarius, 21, 81, 88–89
  candle magick and, 151
Aries, 21, 81
  candle magick and, 150, 151
Artists, case studies, 72–73
  graphic, 57–58
"As above, so below," xix, 20, 184
Astral assistants (beings), 135, 140
Astral plane, 135, 142–45
  author's experience, 183–86
Astrology, 20–22, 75–89
  candle magick and, 151
  case studies, xvii–xviii, 78–80, 87–88
  charting yourself, 84
  elements and aspects, 83
  houses and personal effects, 82
  incense and, 157

Astrology (*cont.*)
  master table, 85–86
  quick reference chart, 86
  recommended reading, 196
  ruling planets, 21, 81–82
  signs, 21, 81
  Web site, 193
Athena, 5–6
Attire. *See* Work attire
Attorney, case study, 63–64
Ayza, 98

Backstabbers, Santeria for, 123–25
Banishing Ritual of the Lesser
    Pentagram, 14–15
Baron Samedi, 98
Barr, Roseanne, 18
Baruch, Bernard, 138
Basic steps, xxii–xxiii, 23–24,
    26–39
  honing sixth sense, 26–30
Beast 666, 15, 163
Beeswax candles, 149, 192
Belief in magick, xviii
  charms, 61–62
  reaffirming, xxiii–xxiv
*Bell, Book and Candle* (movie),
    169–70
Beltane, 173
Benzoin, 158
Bergamot, 158
Bernhard, Sandra, 18
Bibliography, 197–202
Big guardian angels, 12
Binah, 137
Black candles, 45, 151
Black lamp, 93–94
Black magick, xxii–xxiii, 177
  voodoo and, 12
Black rag doll, 123–25
"Blessed be," 4
Blue candles, 45, 151
Boss-fix oil, 45, 189–90
*Botanica,* 107, 117
Bracelets, 174
Brown candles, 151
Buckland, Raymond, 8, 194
*Buckland's Complete Book of
    Witchcraft,* 8, 194
Buckthorn, 153
Budgets, spell casting for, 48, 56

Business, why magick works in,
    xvi–xviii
Business attire, 171–74
  conservative, 173–74, 175
  liberal, 171–72, 175
  relaxed, 172–73, 175
Business capital, Santeria for,
    118–21
Business personality, 175–79. *See
    also* Magickal persona
Business problems, *loa* lamps and
    bottles for, 102
Business prosperity. *See* Prosperity
Business strategy, spell casting for,
    48, 56
Business street smarts, 180–81
Business success
  John the Conqueror root for, 153
  powders and oils for, 45
  triple spell for, 159–60

Cabal. *See* Corporate Magick Cabal
Cabala. *See* Kabbalah
Cabot, Laurie, 41–42
Cancer, 21, 81
  candle magick and, 151
Candle dressings, 191–92
Candles (candle spells), 45, 148–52
  author's experience with,
      186–87, 188–89
  case study, 57–58
  chart for, 151
  colors, 45, 150, 151
  for consecrating office space,
      36–37
  flame interpretation, 151–52
  general tips for using, 149–50
  how-to tips, 191–92
  for prosperity, 109–10
  recommended reading, 195
  for stock market, 122–23
Capricorn, 21, 81
  candle magick and, 151
Career advancement
  author's experience, 181–88
  bergamot incense for, 158
  *juju* for, 99
  Kabbalah for, case study, 131–34
  spell casting for, 48, 56–57
Carnegie, Andrew, 140
Case studies

Allen (attorney), 63–64
Amy (florist), 50–51
Bill (stock broker), 154–55
Bill and Tiffany (artists), 72–73
Diana (designer), 87–88
Fae (Internet entrepreneur),
    94–96
Jenny (editor in chief), 41–43
Margot Adler, 5–6
Michael (management consul-
    tant), 78–80
Mike (stock trader), 13–14
Morris (car salesperson), 66–67
Phyllis (real estate broker),
    18–19
Robin (advertising), 131–34
Rose (graphic artist), 57–58
Sandra (dog walker), 154
Sarah (accountant), 69–70
Scott (salesperson), 53–54
Catholic saints
    Santeria and, 8–9, 31, 105, 106
    voodoo and, 11–12, 91–92
Censers, 156
Cernunnos, 8
Chango, 9, 113–16
    Victory Oil Lamp, 114, 115–16
Charisma, 161–63, 176
Charms, 61–63
    case study, 63–64
    Instant Magick Index Card, 65
    voodoo, 93–94, 99–104
Chesed, 137
Chicken's-foot fetish, case study,
    69–70
Chokmah, 137
Chopra, Deepak, xx
Christianity, 8, 9, 128, 155. *See also*
    Catholic saints
Cinnamon, 158
Circles for protection, 38
Clarity, Santeria for, 111–13
Clothing, 171–74
    conservative, 173–74, 175
    liberal, 171–72, 175
    relaxed, 172–73, 175
Clove, 13–14, 158
Clover, 153
Coca-Cola, 75–76
Colors
    of candles, 45, 150, 151

Kabbalah and, 17–18, 137,
    138–39
    for office space, 167, 169
Command powder, 56
Communication problems, Santeria
    for, 109–10
Competition, *mojo* for, 101
Concentration, absolute, 24–25.
    *See also* Sixth sense
Consecrating office space, 36–37
Conservative office space, 169–70
Conservative work attire, 173–74,
    175
Corner office. *See* Office
Corporate, use of term, xii–xiii
Corporate backstabbers, Santeria
    for, 123–25
Corporate Magick Cabal, xii
    amulets, 74
    charms, 65
    fetishes, 71
    spells, 60
    talismans, 68
Corporate Magick Web site, xii
Counterintelligence, *mojo* for, 101
Craft, the. *See* Witchcraft
Creation, Father of (Obatala), 9,
    111–13
Creativity block, Santeria for,
    111–13
Crone, the, 7
Crow Haven Corner (Salem),
    41–42
Crowley, Aleister, xx, 15, 34, 163,
    185

Danbhala, 12, 98
Dark/light room exercise, 26–27
Days and hours, spell casting and,
    46
Declining moon, 46
Defense, *mojo* for, 101
Deities. *See* Goddesses and gods
Déjà vu, xix–xx
Demeanor, 175–79
Devil's shoestring, 153
Diana, 7
Dirt spell, to eliminate someone,
    117–18
Disciplines, 3–22. *See also specific
    disciplines*

Divine Messenger (Elleggua), 9,
    107–10
Dolls
    black rag, 123–25
    poppet, 55, 188–89, 192
    voodoo, 11, 91, 94–96, 103
Dragon's blood reed, 9, 153
Drawing down the moon, 38
*Drawing Down the Moon* (Adler),
    5, 6
Dress. *See* Work attire
Dunwich, Gerina, *Modern Witch's
    Complete Sourcebook,* 192
Dyer, Wayne W., xx

Earth
    astrology and, 21, 83
    incense and, 155
*Ebo* (offerings), 98, 112
Eliminating someone, dirt spell for,
    117–18
Elleggua, 9, 107–10
    spell to, 109–10
Employee firing, Santeria for,
    116–18
Energy directors, for spells, 45, 52
Energy flow, 32–33
    Kabbalah and, 135, 140–42
Ephemerides, 22, 84, 85
Evil eye, 155
Exercise, for honing sixth sense,
    26–30
Ezili, 98

Faith in magick, xxi. *See also* Belief
    in magick
Father of Creation (Obatala), 9,
    111–13
*Feitico,* 68
Fetishes, 62, 68–69
    black rag doll, 123–25
    case study, 69–70
    Instant Magick Index Card, 71
Finances
    clove incense for, 158
    clover for, 153
    *gris-gris* for, 100
    Santeria for, 118–21
Fire, 148. *See also* Candles
    astrology and, 21, 83
    incense and, 155

Firing employee, Santeria for,
    116–18
Flaming Sword, 141
Florist, case study, 50–51
Focusing, 24–26. *See also* Sixth
    sense
Food, in Santeria, 10
Frankincense, 158
Furnishing office space, 35–36,
    167, 169

Gardenia oil, 112–13
Gardner, Gerald B. (Gardnerian
    witchcraft), 7
Geburah, 136, 137, 141
*Gematria,* Kabbalah and, 16–17,
    128
Gemini, xviii, 21, 81
    candle magick and, 151
Gender, use of in book, xiii
Ginger, 158
Goddesses and gods. *See also specific
    goddesses and gods*
    astrology and, 21
    Santeria. See *Orishas*
    voodoo *(loas),* 12, 93, 96–98
    witchcraft and, 4, 7, 8
Golden Dawn, 15, 128
*Golden Secrets of Mystic Oils* (Riva),
    36
Goodwin, Marcus, *The Psychic
    Investor,* xviii, 20, 75, 85
"Goth" clothing, 172
Graphic artist, case study, 57–58
Gray candles, 151
Green candles, 45, 151, 187
Grimoires, 38, 46, 189
*Gris-gris* bags, 12–13, 62, 99, 100
    case studies, 63–64, 94–96
    preparing, 100

"Hand of Glory," 71, 149
Hearst, William Randolph, 144
Herbs, 152–54
    for black doll (Yemaya), 124–25
    for candle spell (Orunla), 122–23
    case study, 154
    for *gris-gris,* 100
    for magickal pouch amulet
        (Obatala), 112–13
    mail-order supplies, 194

for obtaining money (Oshun),
120–21
for prosperity candle (Elleggua),
109–10
recommended reading, 195
ten essential, 152–54
for victory oil lamp (Chango),
115–16
Hermetic Kabbalah, 14, 15, 127
High John the Conqueror, 45, 55,
56, 153
High magick, 47
Hill, Napoleon, 138
Hod, 132–34, 137
Horoscopes. *See* Astrology
Hostile takeovers, Santeria for,
113–16
Hours and days, spell casting and,
46
Houses, astrology and, 82
How-to tips, 191–92

Identifying
your astral assistant, in Kabbalah,
135, 140
your sacred space, 35
Incense, 155–58
case study, 158–59
four elements and, 155
in offices, 167–68
for purification, 37
recommended reading, 195
senses and, 155–56
for spells, 45
ten essential, 156–57, 158
Index cards. *See* Instant Magick
Index Cards
Information sources, 192–93
Instant Magick Index Cards, xii
amulets, 73–74
charms, 65
cultivating magician's demeanor,
179
fetishes, 71
Kabbalah, 146
office, 170
Santeria spell, 125
spell casting, 59
spell for business success and
guidance, 159–60
talismans, 67–68

voodoo charms, 104
work attire, 175
Internet sources, 192–93

Jewelry, 174–75
Job advancement
author's experience, 181–88
bergamot incense for, 158
*juju* for, 99
spell casting for, 48, 56–57
John the Conqueror, 45, 55, 56,
153
Judaism, 92, 127. *See also* Kabbalah
*Juju*, 99, 100
Jupiter, 21, 38, 46, 82

Kabbalah, 14–18, 126–46
asking for help, 135, 142–44
background and history, 15,
127–28
case studies, 18–19, 131–34
choosing a sphere, 135, 136–37
creating yourself as master, 135,
144–45
identifying your astral assistant,
135, 140
Instant Magick Index Card, 146
practical advantages of, 129–31
preparing, 135, 138–39
recommended reading, 196
steps for using, 135
Web site, 193
white light and, 32
working the energy, 135, 140–42
yoga and, 131
Kether, 137
*Keys to the Mysteries* (Levi), 15
Korda, Michael, *Success!*, 165–66

Labor God (Oggun), 9, 116–18
LaVey, Anton Szandor, 8, 196
Lawyer, case study, 63–64
Left-hand path, xxii
Legal matters, buckthorn for, 153
Lemon balm, 158
Leo, 21, 81
candle magick and, 151
Levi, Eliphas (Alphonse Louis
Constant), 15
Liberal work attire, 171–72, 175
Libra, 21, 81

Libra (*cont.*)
  candle magick and, 151
Light/dark room exercise, 26–27
Lighting, for office space, 167, 169
"Like produces like," 44
Little guardian angels, 12
*Loa* lamps and bottles, 102
Loans (financing)
  *gris-gris* for, 100
  Santeria for, 118–21
*Loas* (voodoo gods), 12, 93, 96–98
Lovage, 153
Low magick, 6–7, 40, 43, 47
Lucky charms. *See* Charms;
  Talismans

McCormack, Mark, *What They
  Don't Teach You at Harvard
  Business School,* 180
Mackay, Harvey, *Swim With the
  Sharks Without Being Eaten
  Alive,* 180
Madonna, 18
Magazine publishing
  author's experience, 181–90
  case study, 41–43
Magick
  in business, xvi–xviii
  how it works, xviii–xx
  schools of, 3–22. *See also specific
    schools*
  three basic steps of, xxii–xxiii,
    23–24
  white versus black, xxii
Magickal attire, 171–74
  conservative, 173–74, 175
  liberal, 171–72, 175
  relaxed, 172–73, 175
Magickal demeanor, 175–79
Magickal herbs. *See* Herbs
Magickal office. *See* Office
Magickal persona, 163–65
  clothing, 171–74
  creating your, 30–33
  demeanor and, 175–79
  jewelry, 174–75
  office space and, 165–70
Magickal pouch amulet, 112–13
Maiden, the, 7
Mail-order supplies, 194
Malkuth, 16, 17, 19, 130, 136,
  137, 146, 152

Management
  astrology for, case study, 78–80
  of long distance staff, Santeria
    for, 107–10
  mandrake root for, 153
Mandino, Og, 140
Mandrake root, 153
Mantras, 49, 141–42, 184–85
Marasa, 98
Mars, 21, 82
Mawu Lisa, 98
*Mayombero,* 119
Meditation, 48–49, 129, 139. *See
  also* Sixth sense
Meetings
  *gris-gris* for, 100
  spell casting for, 47, 52–53
Mercury, 21, 81
Messenger (voodoo) dolls, 11, 91,
  103
  case studies, 13–14, 94–96
*Mezuzah,* 92
Michael, Archangel, 16, 132–34,
  140
Middle Pillar of Light, 32
Millionaire oil, 45, 56
Mind-body connection, xx
Mind control, xx, 24–25. *See also*
  Sixth sense
*Modern Witch's Complete Sourcebook*
  (Dunwich), 192
*Mojo* bags, 12–13, 99, 101
  case study, 63–64
  preparing, 101
Money. *See also* Finances
  Santeria spells for obtaining,
    120–21
  snakeroot for, 154
Money Goddess (Oshun), 9, 10,
  118–21
Moon (moon cycles), 21, 81
  astrology and, 77
  spell casting and, 46
Morgan, J. P., xviii, 76
Moses, 11–12, 126, 127
Mother, the, 7
Mugwort, 154
Mundane astrology, 21, 77
Myrrh, 158
*Mysteres. See Loas*
Mysterious magician's office,
  168–69, 170

Natal astrology, 21, 77
National Public Radio (NPR), 5
Necromancy, 71, 149
Negative presence, purifying, 37
Negotiations, *gris-gris* for, 100
Neptune, 21, 82
Netzach, 137
Numbers, Kabbalah and, 16–17, 128
Nutmeg, 109–10

Obatala, 9, 111–13
    spell to, 112–13
Occult jewelry, 174–75
Offerings, 96–97, 98, 112
Office, 165–70
    consecrating, 36–37
    environments, 166–70
    furnishing, 35–36
    identifying space, 35
    Instant Magick Index Card, 170
    mysterious magician's, 168–69, 170
    preparing your, 33–38, 168
    private magician's, 169–70
    protecting, 37–38
    proud magician's, 166–68, 170
Office backstabbers, Santeria for, 123–25
Oggun, 9, 116–18
    dirt spell to, 117–18
Ogilvy, David, 36
Ogou, 98
Oil lamps, 114, 115–16
Oils, 153
    candle magick and, 150, 151
    incense and, 157
    making your own, 191
    recommended reading, 195
    for spells, 45
Olive candles, 151
Olodunare, 105
Onyx stone, 88
Orange candles, 151, 186–87
*Orishas,* 9, 105, 106, 107–25
    Chango, 9, 113–16
    Elleggua, 9, 107–10
    Obatala, 9, 111–13
    Oggun, 9, 116–18
    Orunla, 9, 121–23
    Oshun, 9, 10, 118–21
    Yemaya, 9, 123–25

Orunla, 9, 121–23
    candle spell to, 122–23
Oshun, 9, 10, 118–21
    spells to, 120–21
Outing yourself, 163–65
    proud magician's office, 166–68, 170
Outward demeanor, 175–79

Pagan altars, 51, 97
    preparing, 33–38
Paganism, 4, 5
*Paket Kongo,* 99, 101–2
*Palo monte,* 114, 115
*Palos,* 106
Pan, 8
Papa Legba, 12, 98
Partnerships
    *juju* for, 100
    sweet pea for, 154
Patchouli, 45, 157
Path of the Flaming Sword, 141
Path of Wisdom, 17
Patience stones, 72–73
Peale, Norman Vincent, xx
Pentagrams, 166, 174
    concentration exercise, 27–29
Peony, 158
Persona, 163–65
    clothing, 171–74
    creating your, 30–33
    demeanor and, 175–79
    jewelry, 174–75
    office space and, 165–70
Personnel
    astrology for, 86
    bergamot incense for, 158
    *gris-gris* for, 100
    spell casting for, 47–48, 55
Pisces, 21, 81
    candle magick and, 151
Pluto, 21, 82
Pomegranate, 115–16
Poppet dolls, 55, 188–89
    case study, 13–14
    how-to tips, 192
Powders, for spells, 45
Power brokers, 31
Power God (Chango), 9, 113–16
Power office. *See* Office
Power persona. *See* Persona
Preparation, 23–39, 184

210    *Index*

Preparation (*cont.*)
  creating your power persona,
    30–33
  focusing, 25–26
  honing your sixth sense, 26–30
  for Kabbalah, 138–39
  of office space, 33–38, 168
  for spells, 48–50
  three steps of, 26–39
Presentations, *gris-gris* for, 100
Private magician's office, 169–70
Progressive work environment
  liberal work attire for, 171–72,
    175
  proud magician's office for,
    166–68, 170
Projects, spell casting for, 47, 52
Prophecy God (Orunla), 9, 121–23
Prosperity, benzoin incense for, 158
Prosperity candle, 109–10
Prosperity spells, 125
  case study, 42–43
Protection
  dragon's blood reed for, 153
  *mojo* for, 101
  powders and oils for, 45
  of sacred space, 37–38
Protection Goddess (Yemaya), 9,
  123–25
Proud magician's office, 166–68,
  170
*Psychic Investor, The* (Goodwin),
  xviii, 20, 75, 85
Publishing
  author's experience, 181–90
  case study, 41–43
Purification incense, 37
Purple candles, 151, 186–87

Qabala. *See* Kabbalah
Quick fixes, thunderstones for,
  102–3

Rainbow candles, 151
Raises, *juju* for, 100
Ravens, 53–54
Reading, recommended, 194–96
Reaffirming your beliefs, xxiii–xxiv
Real estate broker, case study,
  18–19
Red candles, 45, 150, 151
*Regla de ocha. See* Santeria

Relaxed work attire, 172–73, 175
Resources, 191–96
Right-hand path, xxii
Ritual of the Lesser Pentagram,
  14–15
Riva, Anna, *Golden Secrets of Mystic
  Oils,* 36
Robbins, Anthony, xx, 138
Roman Catholic saints
  Santeria and, 8–9, 31, 105, 106
  voodoo and, 11–12, 91–92

Sabbats, 7, 173
Sacred space. *See also* Office
  preparing, 33–38
Sacrifice
  Santeria and, 9, 10, 106, 119
  voodoo and, 96–97
Sagittarius, 21, 81
  candle magick and, 151
Sales
  *juju* for, 100
  lemon balm incense for, 158
  lovage for, 153
Salespeople, case studies, 53–54,
  66–67
Salt water, 37
Sandalwood, 158, 159
Santeria, 8–11, 105–25. *See also*
  Santeria spells
  candle interpretations and,
    151–52
  case studies, 10, 107–25
  Chango, 9, 113–16
  Elleggua, 9, 107–10
  Instant Magick Index Card, 125
  Obatala, 9, 111–13
  Oggun, 9, 116–18
  Orunla, 9, 121–23
  Oshun, 9, 10, 118–21
  recommended reading, 195
  Yemaya, 9, 123–25
Santeria spells, 9, 107
  for communication problems,
    109–10
  for creativity block, 112–13
  to eliminate someone, 117–18
  for general business prosperity,
    125
  for hostile takeovers, 115–16
  for obtaining money, 120–21
  for stock market, 122–23

for stopping backstabbers,
123–25
*Santeros/santeras,* 9, 105–6
Satan (Satanism), 8, 149, 193, 196
Saturn, 21, 82
Schools of magick, 3–22. *See also*
*specific disciplines*
Science, magick and, xix–xx
Scorpio, 21, 81
candle magick and, 151
Scrying mirrors, 50–51
Seax-Wica, 8
Self-confidence, 164
Sephiroth (Sephira), 15–19,
128–30
asking for help, 135, 142–44
case study, 131–34
choosing a sphere, 135, 136–37
creating yourself as master, 135,
144–45
preparing, 138–39
working the energy, 135,
140–42
Seven African Powers, 9, 107–25
Chango, 9, 113–16
Elleggua, 9, 107–10
Obatala, 9, 111–13
Oggun, 9, 116–18
Orunla, 9, 121–23
Oshun, 9, 10, 118–21
Yemaya, 9, 123–25
*777* (Crowely), 15
Silva, Jose, xx, 186
Six statements, xxiii–xxiv, 23–24
Sixth sense, 24–25, 48–49
honing your, 26–30
Snakeroot, 154
Spells, 40–60
for budgets or gathering money,
48, 56
for business strategy, 48, 56
for career advancement, 48,
56–57
case studies, 41–43, 50–51,
53–54, 57–58
for completing projects, 47, 52
Instant Magick Index Card for,
59
for meetings, 47, 52–53
for personnel matters, 47–48, 55
preparing for, 48–50
Santeria. *See* Santeria spells

six business scenarios, 47–48
timing, 46
tools for, 45–46, 148–59
what you need, 44–46
Spiritual guardians, 31
Splendid Lights. *See* Sephiroth
Stock market
astrology for, xvii–xviii, 85
candle spells for, case study,
57–58
mugwort for, 154
Santeria for, 121–23
voodoo for, case study, 13–14
Street smarts, 180–81
Subconscious, 48–50, 183–84
Success
John the Conqueror root for,
153
powders and oils for, 45
triple spell for, 159–60
*Success!* (Korda), 165–66
Success oil, 45, 52–53, 56, 187
Sudden tasks, thunderstones for,
102–3
Suffumigation, 157
Sun, 21, 81
Sunday, astrology and, 46
Supplies, 193, 194
Sweet pea, 154
*Swim With the Sharks Without Being
Eaten Alive* (Mackay), 180

Talismans, 61–63, 65
case study, 66–67
definition of, 62–63, 71
Instant Magick Index Card,
67–68
for spells, 45
Tallow (lard) candles, 149, 192
Taurus, 21, 78–80, 81
candle magick and, 151
Telephone interview, case study,
5–6
Terminations, dirt spell for, 117–18
Third eye, 24–25
Thoth, 128
Three basic steps, xxii–xxiii, 23–24,
26–39
honing sixth sense, 26–30
Thunderstones, 102–3
Thursday, astrology and, 46
Timing spells, 46

Tiphareth, 137, 146
Tools, 147–60. *See also* Candles;
     Herbs; Incense
  resources for, 193, 194
  for spells, 45–46, 148–59
Torah, 127
*Transcendental Magic* (Levi), 15
Tree of Life (Kabbalah), 15–19,
     128–30
  asking for help, 135, 142–44
  case study, 131–34
  choosing a sphere, 135, 136–37
  creating yourself as master, 135,
     144–45
  preparing, 138–39
  working the energy, 135, 140–42
Tree stick, 114, 115
Trismegistus, Hermes, 128
Troublemakers, Santeria for,
     123–25
Trump, Donald, 31, 138

Universal plane, xix
Uranus, 21, 82

Vampires, 57–58
Venus, 21, 81
Victory Oil Lamp, 114, 115–16
Violet candles, 151, 186–87
Virgo, 21, 81
  candle magick and, 151
Virulent imagination, 49–50
Visualization, xx, 25, 37, 49–50,
     183
Voodoo (Voudon), 11–13, 90–104
  case studies, 13–14, 94–96
  charms, 93–94, 99–104
  Instant Magick Index Card, 104
  *loas*, 12, 93, 96–98
  recommended reading, 195
  using at work, 97–98
  Web site, 193
Voodoo dolls, 11, 91, 103
  case studies, 13–14, 94–96

Wall Street. *See* Stock market
*Wall Street Journal*, 68

Waning moon, 46
Wardrobe. *See* Work attire
Waxing moon, 46, 72–73
Wealthy Way powder, 45, 56
Web sites, 192–93
  Corporate Magick, xii
Wednesday, astrology and, 46
Western Mystery Tradition, 128
*What They Don't Teach You at
     Harvard Business School*
     (McCormack), 180
White candles, 36–37, 151
White light, 32–33
White magick, xxii–xxiii
  Santeria and, 9
Wicca. *See* Witchcraft
*Wiccan Web, The* (Telesco and
     Knight), 192
Willpower oil, 45, 56
Wind, astrology and, 21, 83
Winfrey, Oprah, 31
Witchcraft (Wicca), 4, 6–8. *See also*
     Spells
  case study, 5–6
  recommended reading, 194
  Web site, 193
Work attire, 171–74
  conservative, 173–74, 175
  liberal, 171–72, 175
  relaxed, 172–73, 175
Work environment. *See* Office
Work self, 175–76. *See also*
     Magickal persona
Work space. *See* Office

Yellow candles, 151
Yemaya, 9, 123–25
  black rag doll, 124–25
Yesod, 137
Yoga, Kabbalah and, 131
Yoruba tribes, Santeria and, 9

Zaka, 96, 98
Zodiac, 21–22, 76–77, 78. *See also*
     Astrology
Zombies, 12